HMS

LOG BOOK

Natalie! Thank you for gift your precious gift to the world! Jen

HMS LOG BOOK

JULY - DECEMBER 2019

MIND • SPIRIT • BODY
JOURNAL

JENNIFER M SNYDER

—

CREATESPACE SOUTH CAROLINA

WWW.HMSLOGBOOK.COM

Contents

Part One

Circle of Captains

Some very important women have come to the Captain's Circle over the years with their love, guidance, wisdom, grace and healing energy. They are the women who inspired the creation of the HMS Log Book. We give abundant love and gratitude to all the family and friends who continue to support this journey. The pages of the journal are dripping with your encouragement and enthusiasm, and we couldn't do this without you.

With this ninth edition of the journal, we embark on the fifth year of this voyage of self-discovery. To those who have been with us from the beginning we give a heart-felt thank you. To those who are just joining us, we are so happy to have you on board. Please take some time to get to know the journal by reading the following introductory pages. Here you will find an in-depth discussion on the how's, the why's and the what's that may come up as you dive into the journal. This experience is a very unique self-awareness tool, so we encourage you to get familiar with the wide range of aspects included in this guided journaling process.

A very special thank you to Mystic Mamma,
Divine Curator of the most inspirational writers of the day.

The HMS Log Book is dedicated to Madeline Grace,
the bravest Captain of them all.

Introduction

It is in the tradition of ancient mariners' logs that the HMS Log Book is crafted. A ship's log is a meticulous record of vital statistics that the captain, crew, and vessel experience along their journey. A typical log book documented the weather; the position of the stars & moon; crew morale; inventories of food, drink, & merchandise; activities; excursions; curiosities, and so on. The process is an old one, a practical exercise whereby a Captain becomes intimately acquainted with the ship.

Today's feminine mariner is the embodiment of a magnificent vessel. Her mind is the captain; her body, the ship; and her soul, the crew. She is a dynamic trio on a fantastic journey across the waters of time, and hers is a voyage worth documenting. The modern captain, operating a tight ship with an even tighter schedule, requires a journal that provides the framework to quickly and efficiently record the statistics of her daily journey.

Her Majesty's Sovereign Log Book

The HMS Log Book is a fill-in-the-blank, daily journal designed to capture all that a woman encounters on her journey. Each page of the Log Book presents the current moon phase along with the current astrological phase, elemental phase, and season. Against this celestial backdrop, the Captain logs the weather; hours of sleep; exercise & meditation; quantities of food, water, alcohol & medication consumed; stress levels; challenges; daily intentions & gratitude; and menses & moods. The Log Book encompasses all the essential details of a woman's life in a smart, concise format that becomes a daily snapshot of her mind, body, and soul. As the pages of the Log Book are studied over time, the patterns and life cycles become easy to identify.

The HMS Log Book invites a woman to take stock of her life and chart the details in an intimate and beautiful forum. It inspires her to have a moment with the moon and stars while pondering the elements of the day, the state of Her Majesty's Ship, and the conditions under which she is traveling. It becomes a ritual of focusing on the mind, body, and spirit while connecting with the rhythm of Earth and the Heavens. And most importantly, the HMS Log Book provides powerful opportunities for raising self-awareness from stern to bow. Bon Voyage!

Legend

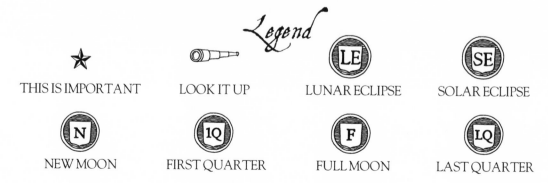

| THIS IS IMPORTANT | LOOK IT UP | LUNAR ECLIPSE | SOLAR ECLIPSE |
| NEW MOON | FIRST QUARTER | FULL MOON | LAST QUARTER |

Captain's Oath

 For the admiral, water dog, or pirate alike, every departure on a sea-faring vessel must be preceded by the signing of The Code. The Captain's code will briefly outline the rules of conduct, and the resulting consequences for all parties while out to sea. The Chasse-Partie, or "hunting party," for example, is an old term used to describe a pirate's code for dealing with such things as rowdy behavior, mutiny, dividing the bounty, and outlining which actions warrant a marooning. It is in the tradition of both the unsavory scalawag and the venerable four-striper of days gone by that the Captains present this code for all who begin their voyage with the HMS Log Book. Keep to The Code, and you will receive maximum benefit from your new life management tool.

On my Honor, I pledge and I swear that...

I will enter into the daily ritual of the Log Book with a true and open heart. Without judgment, guilt, or shame, I will record my daily activities for scientific purposes only.

I will use the data gathered herein to raise awareness of my daily habits and the consequences they garner. I will always tend to this task with loving kindness for my spirit and all those whom I encounter.

I will strive to maintain a safety zone within the log book, and in my review of the data, I will always be constructive and emotionally neutral. I will remember that it is my duty to format the document with love, patience, forgiveness, understanding, peace, and positive energy.

I will aim to abide by The Code, but I will always remember that I am doing the very best I can at the moment, and that every tomorrow is a new opportunity to make healthy choices for my mind, body, and spirit.

Signature

We Have an Accord

The Log Book, Deconstructed

"And God said, 'Let there be lights in the expanse of the heavens to separate the day from the night. And let them be for signs...'" Genesis 1:14

If we consider the Captains of a few centuries ago and their movement across the waters of the globe, one thing we could certainly presume is that these folks had a complete and total understanding of the movement of Earth's celestial bodies. This knowledge was imperative to the success of every voyage from the beginning of time to the recent development of sophisticated systems. For centuries, Captains have been looking up, and we like that.

In the same way that the stars have guided sailors, Wise Men, and Prophets through their journeys, we contend that the modern mariner can also greatly benefit from an awareness of these cycles. For instance, the moon moves the oceans, significantly. In the most southerly and northerly ports, the waters rise and fall a staggering fifty feet in a single day. We think it safe to presume that the moon also moves our little individual bodies of water. We are microscopic compared to the vast energy of the oceans and much more easily swayed.

We are affected by the moon, and a daily awareness of the movement of this celestial body will enhance your life. The moon is front and center in the pages of the Log Book for this reason, and we hope that you will delight in the understanding of its influence. Take a tip from your ancestors and look up; there is much to be learned from the night sky. We propose that you travel with an awareness of the moon & constellations and find calmer seas for it.

Volumes have been written on the subject of astrology, and if this topic interests you, we encourage you to do some research. We recommend starting with SkyWatch Astrology at www.skywatchastrology. com. These folks will guide you through your day with a forecast on how the stars are affecting the herd. You will not find your horoscope on this website, only a more useful heads up on the energy that will be affecting you and the people in your landscape. If you are new to astrology and need a little more explanation than Lance and Leslie provide, head on over to Cafe Astrology at www.cafeastrology.com. The Captains like these two sites for their usability and relevance.

If you crave a more in depth explanation of the current Astrology the Captains suggest you check out The Pele Report with Kaypacha at www.newparadigmastrology.com. His brilliant insight and abundant humor make this weekly forecast a must see for folks across the globe. The next few pages provide a brief overview of the basics but come nowhere near to encompassing the vast well of data that is available. After all, humans have studied the heavens for a very, very long time.

The Moon

The farmers of yesteryear knew to plant their crops on the New Moon so that the seeds would grow with the moon. This is ancient knowledge, only recently forgotten by the agricultural industry. This was practiced for centuries because it is effective, and we are all about effective. Now if we translate this idea into everyday life, we begin to understand that while the New Moon is a great time to start a project or task, the Full Moon is the time to think about closing or finishing projects. We identify the energy in the air and schedule accordingly. As we follow the phases of the moon and become aware of its waxing & waning cycles, we can plan our journey with a little more precision and a lot more success.

The Eclipses

A solar eclipse occurs when the moon blocks the sun. This lunation is a very potent time in the grand cycle of life and always occurs at a new moon. Sarah Varcas, at Astro-Awakenings.com, says a solar eclipse "...functions in some ways like a super charged New Moon. So we need to find every bit of fuel and fertilizer inside us, which basically means energy in all its forms (thoughts, emotions, instincts, intuition, physicality) and invest it now in this moment of intense creativity. The seeds that we plant in our lives at a solar eclipse will grow strong and vibrant." [1] Take advantage of this opportunity to create and transform. It is the gift of beginnings.

A lunar eclipse occurs when the moon passes directly behind the Earth into its umbra, or shadow. This lunation is also a very potent time, but for different reasons. Dipali Desai, via www.mysticmamma.com, offers this advice: "Lunar Eclipses symbolize an ending of a chapter, time of letting go, surrendering and closing of doors so to speak. You can see this is a great time of shedding the past, at least whatever you are ready to, and really diving into it and letting go. Don't over-analyze it. Release the grip and set yourself free to heal and move on. Honor whatever it is or was and let it go on all levels of your being." [2] Another nugget found at the gold mine that is the Mystic Mamma site comes from Cathy Pagano: "Lunar eclipses (which have a 19 year cycle) signal a completion and an awareness that could change the course of our journey if we let it.... May you finally get the message and leave the past behind, honoring the experiences by making them conscious and giving them meaning..." [3] Take advantage of this opportunity to release and recover. It is the gift of endings.

The zodiac

For the purpose of the Log Book, we will consider how the astrological sign and its corresponding element and quality impact our energy field. Taking the first sign of the Zodiac, Aries (March 21-April 20), as an example, consider how this is a time of intense energy, as spring bursts forth with new life. Aries is the fire element, and you can understand why. It takes quite a bit of energy to wake up from the slumber of winter, and this is a time when inspiration, manifestation, and even a touch of agitation are palpable. The energy quickens with the Spring Equinox, and everything really begins to move. Add to this the fact that Aries is a cardinal sign, which translates as spontaneity and leadership, and you can see these qualities become even more intensified. Now for contrast, look at Pisces, the last sign of the Zodiac. Occurring in late winter, Pisces is a water sign with a mutable quality, making it a time of slow motion, inward orientation, and easy-going energy. Whereas Aries is dynamic & explosive, Pisces is mature & deliberate. Goldschneider and Elffers, in The Secret Language of Birthdays, provide the following description of the elements and qualities of the signs:

The four elements in the Zodiac are:

- Fire -a time of enthusiasm, passion, inspiration, and all forms of outward emotional expression [4] {Up, like a sprout from the soil}
- Earth -a time of grounding energy, practical concerns, tangible results, and mental expression [4] {Down, like roots through the ground}
- Air - a time of intellectual, objective & abstract energy, and mental expression [4] {Out, like thoughts from the mind}
- Water - a time of personal, internal & feeling-oriented energy, and emotional expression [4] {In, like diving deep inside ourselves}

The three qualities in the Zodiac are:

- Cardinal ~ physical activity, spontaneity, leadership, and independence
- Fixed ~ follow-through, stability, loyalty, determination, and inflexibility
- Mutable ~ adaptability, spontaneous adjustment, and smooth sailing [5]

The Captains have found that even a minor understanding of these concepts can positively impact the journey, so the day's constellation and elemental sign are included on each page of the Log Book. You will also find that at the beginning of each astrological sign, a Zodiac "Fact Sheet" is included to give you a brief overview of the sign and its aspects.

Signs of the Zodiac

♈	Aries – Fire – Cardinal		♎	Libra – Air – Cardinal
♉	Taurus – Earth – Fixed		♏	Scorpio – Water – Fixed
♊	Gemini – Air – Mutable		♐	Sagittarius – Fire – Mutable
♋	Cancer – Water – Cardinal		♑	Capricorn – Earth – Cardinal
♌	Leo – Fire – Fixed		♒	Aquarius – Air – Fixed
♍	Virgo – Earth – Mutable		♓	Pisces – Water – Mutable

The Seasons

"To everything there is a season, and a time to every purpose under Heaven,"
Ecclesiastes 3:1

"Turn, turn, turn. . ." In order to visually pay homage to this notion, each day of the Log Book depicts the same tree in varying stages of life. Let this tree serve as a daily reminder of the broad, slow-moving cycle of our beautiful planet, and let this ritual inspire you to slow down and slip gently into the rhythm of Earth & the Heavens.

Part Two

Intention

Right at this very moment, the universe is conspiring to deliver all the resources you will need to sing your song. It will provide the string section, the percussion & brass sections, the music & the stands, the conductor, the performance hall, the lights, the tickets, and the audience. The universe will happily send along a magnificent dress, hair & make-up artists, back up dancers (if you really need them), and the champagne toast for when you bring the house down. Until you name the tune, however, the universe can only wait with breathless anticipation for your instruction. Boldly state your intention and manifest your reality.

Be specific, include every detail, and believe in yourself. Imagine how you will feel during your time on the stage: feel the wood beneath your feet and the electricity in the air; feel every verse, bar, and rhythm and all the breaths in between. Don't leave anything out. Declare your fee, decide upon the rehearsal schedule, write the press release, design the set, select the invitations, and print the banners. Include all the details, please. With power and love and complete faith, state your intention and manifest your reality.

Set it up, write it down, draw it out ~ then release your intentions to the sea. Let them go and believe that they will manifest. Know that they will manifest. Release control and fear. Resound in the assurance of your success. Practice one pointed awareness so that nothing will distract you from a complete, consistent and detailed visualization of your life once your intentions have manifested.

Play some John Lennon and really "Imagine" how you want to feel. The ultimate goal is to consistently imagine how you will feel within the realm of your success. This process is simple, yet profoundly effective. By switching the focus from "what you want," to "how you want to feel," you instantly change your vibration from attachment to Love. What's the frequency, Kenneth? The frequency is Love. And when you meditate on how you want to feel, with the frequency of Love & non-attachment, you will magnetically attract what you want because you have become it. You are creating within what you want to experience without. You know how this works: like attracts like.

Now it's time to get busy. Action cures fear, and at the same time shows the universe that you are preparing for your intentions to manifest. Can't think what to do? You can't start rehearsing until the orchestra arrives? Then swab the decks, clean the galley, trim the sails, batten down the hatches. Do something productive. Make something happen... anything. The key is to be in motion and action-oriented, with a "rolling stone & no moss" mind-set. Draw the energy into yourself. Give and you will receive.

So while you are peacefully and patiently visualizing your dreams, be sure to pay attention to the signs. They will come in good time. Be open to the messages and the inspiration that come your way. Listen to your inner voice. Really listen. Pay attention to recurring thoughts, and be ever so mindful of the little details in your world. Be sure to give proper thanks when your intuition hits on something that resonates, and know that the Universe is at the wheel with Divine Timing riding shot gun. Then, when the time is right, you may reel it in.

We give you this treasure map, cloaked in a quotation from Charles Haanel, a twentieth century philosopher many refer to as the Father of Personal Development: "The predominant thought or the mental attitude is the magnet, and the law is that like attracts like. Consequently, the mental attitude will invariably attract such conditions as to correspond to its nature."

The Captains recommend logging at least one intention per day. It doesn't have to be life changing or ground-breaking; it only need make sense to you. For example: "I intend to practice non-judgment all day."

Gratitude

The Captains have spent many hours at the Circle, talking, dreaming, ruminating, solving, and circumnavigating. One concept that has never been doubted is the importance of expressing Gratitude on a daily basis. We encourage you to fill this space to the brim.

Meditation

In the grand old days of enlightened celestial navigation, captains relied entirely on the stars, the compass, and a sextant for movement across any open body of water. A sextant is an instrument used to measure the angle between two visible objects, like the moon & Polaris, which makes it an invaluable device for calculating longitude. While latitude is relatively easy to determine, longitude is much more elusive, and until the sextant burst on to the nautical scene early in the 17th century, sailors were seriously vexed by this challenge.

As if navigating the open water weren't difficult enough, our ancestral captains were sailing rather blindfolded. It is all well and good to have the latitude coordinate, but unless you have an accurate longitudinal point, you don't truly know where you are. When you are out to sea, the tiniest longitudinal deviation can have a dramatic effect on the journey. Put enough water between a ship and its destination, and two degrees can mean the difference between Nassau & Norfolk. This navigational issue was such a problem that the British government established The Board of Longitude to find a solution.

As we ponder the challenges of our nautical ancestors, we conclude that the sextant was a tool of the most significant importance and, aside from fresh water, would have been the most valuable item on the ship. With this instrument, longitude was found and captains were liberated.

To our fellow Captains, we encourage you to find your sextant in the ancient practice of mindful meditation. All can sail without a sextant, but with it, as with meditation, you can truly know where you are. Meditation will adjust your perspective from that of the egocentric to a more world-centered view, and this shift naturally leads to greater compassion & love for yourself and others. In the book, Mindfulness: An Eight-Week Plan for Finding Peace in a Frantic World, by Mark Williams and Danny Penman, we find a simple explanation of the benefits of meditation: "In Mindful Meditation, we become aware of our thinking. This pure form of awareness allows us to experience the world directly. It's bigger than thinking. It's unclouded by our thoughts, feelings, and emotions. It's a high vantage point~from which we can see everything for miles around." [6]

It's time to assemble The Board of Longitude in your life. Find your sextant, your high vantage point in the daily practice of meditation, so that you may determine your coordinates. If you feel that you are sailing without direction, without course, and without the proper tools, mindful meditation is an excellent process to help you plot your location on the charts. And when you truly know where you are, it is so much easier to figure out where you are going. Gangway!

Weather

Use this space however you wish. You can stick to the numbers and log the highs and lows or get creative and draw some symbols. Divide the box into AM/PM if you wish, or stick with a summary of the day. The Log Book will come to represent a visual snapshot of your days, so the more imagery you use, the more obvious any patterns will be in review.

Mood

This is what it's all about. All of the variables tracked in the Log Book are responsible for how you feel at the end of the day. Your mood is the sum of these parts, and the Captains believe that this equation is worth studying. If you are feeling off, check out your equation because it's probably out of balance. Again, you may log your mood in whatever way pleases you. We like the number system, but also encourage you to be creative. A smiley face system could be fun.

Sleep

This one is easy. Log your hours and aim for eight.

Cycle

This space is originally intended to track menstrual cycles, but can be used for any type of cycle, even bicycles. If you are tracking your menstrual cycle, you would write "1" for the first day of the cycle. The Captains agree that understanding the relationship between the moon cycle and the menstrual cycle can be very enlightening. The Log Book is therefore designed to make this relationship the focal point of the day. The Life You Were Born To Live, by Dan Millman, offers this insight about cycles:

> Different forms of energy vibrate at different rates like a river; energy flows from higher to lower levels, moving through repeating cycles, expanding then contracting, like our breathing.

> Since everything in the universe is a form of energy, everything falls within the domain of the Law of Cycles: Sunrise and sunset, the waxing and waning moon, the ebb and flow of tides, and the seasons of the year all reflect this law. It reminds us there is a time for everything under the sun. All things rise and fall.

> A thought or action initiated while this pulsing energy is rising, gaining momentum, travels along easily toward its success, but a thought or action initiated in a descending cycle has reduced impact. When a cycle is not favorable we wait until it is rising again. There are times for action and times for stillness, times to talk and times to be silent. Few things are more frustrating than doing the right thing at the wrong time.

> Appreciating the energy cycles of our lives helps us apply good timing and create better "luck" for ourselves. There are times to work and times to rest, times to take advantage of a building cycle and times to go inside, learn patience, and wait, preparing for the next rising wave.

> Each of us has our rhythms. As we find our own rhythm, we take advantage of whatever point of the cycle we find ourselves; we learn to flow in harmony and rhythm with the Law of Cycles. [7]

Water

Keeping the body hydrated is one of the most important responsibilities of a human. Use this space to track how many glasses of water you drink every day. The Captains would like to mention that the quality of your water is just as important. In Secrets of Longevity: Hundreds of Ways to Live to Be 100, Dr. Mao Shing Ni discusses the basics:

> From time immemorial, water has been highly regarded for its therapeutic virtues. Centenarians on every inhabited continent swear by their native water as the source of their long lives. Scientists agree that these particular waters may contribute to the local inhabitants' health and longevity. One thing they all have in common is purity; no chemicals, no toxins. And it's no surprise that these Shangri-las are all located far from any city. Tap water in urban areas contains pesticides, industrial pollutants, chlorine, fluoride, and other chemicals. Well water and mountain streams in some parts of the countryside fare no better due to acid rain and toxic levels of minerals present in groundwater.

> There are many filtration processes that remove contaminants. The best kinds employ activated charcoal, which removes the impurities but leaves the water-soluble minerals. Avoid water softeners, which remove essential minerals, and do not store water in plastic containers, as the PCBs leach into the water. [8]

Throne

So here we are in the guts of the Log Book: Evacuations. Yes, this is a very important function to track. Most holistic practitioners will tell you that your health begins in the gut. If the evacuation route is jammed, unsavory things begin to happen. We've heard tell of some who go three days without proper elimination. This is like carrying dirty diapers around in your purse, but worse. By tracking your "time upon the throne," your awareness of daily cycles will keep you mindful of this very important process. You always want to have at least a "1" in that box, mate.

If this is an issue for you, the Captains suggest reading up on the topic in Healthy Healing by Linda Rector Page. Page is a Ph.D. who offers natural and healthy options for healing the body, including diet & herbal therapy, exercise, vitamin & mineral therapy, acupuncture and many more.

Obstacles

Be mindful that the obstacles you perceive in your life can limit you or set you free. We recommend you not dwell on these perceived obstacles, only that you give them a nod as you navigate around them. List whatever comes to mind and keep to The Code.

The Divine Curator, Mystic Mamma, has offered this channeling of Archangel Michael by Douglas McDaniel, and the Captains wish to pass along this insightful gem to you. The full piece can be found on the Mystic Mamma website, and is most certainly worth the read.

> Now is the time to begin writing the script that will guide the rest of your life, as it unfolds in the journey you are now taking.
>
> Awaken to the possibility. Possibilities are all around you. Take advantage of them and they will shape the next segment of your journey.
>
> The next part of your journey is one of releasing and awareness. You will consciously release all that is not serving you, for you are now not in service just to others, but are in service to yourself as well.
>
> Expand into the new consciousness. Breathe deeply and feel the release of the old energy and the gathering of the new.
>
> The barriers are gone, dear ones, destroyed, no longer needed as obstacles to your spiritual progress. They were once necessary to get your attention, to provide you a chance to focus and realign, but this process is no longer necessary. You are no longer interested in making things difficult and burdensome for yourself.
>
> You are truly interested in the freedom that total enlightenment brings. You are no longer interested in testing yourself to see if you are worthy. You are worthy and are now conscious of that worthiness. [9]

Indulgences

The Captain's Circle makes port in one of the surliest harbors on the Eastern coast, and most of the Captains have had or are currently enjoying their fair share of indulgences. The preferred drink in this fair cove is, "Just one more." It is a city built partially on the Rum Trade during a time when real pirates swung from the gallows in the park, so the party has been happening here for a long time. We get it. The only suggestion is to simply be mindful of these indulgences. Be fully aware of your choices, and recognize each one as that, a choice. As you ponder this, give a nod to the known consequences of whatever the indulgence.

Remember The Code here, and take heart in this little fun fact from Dr. Mao Shing Ni's, Secrets of Longevity: Hundreds of Ways to Live to Be 100: "Extensive research has confirmed the benefits of wine due to its high content of the antioxidant resveratrol. This compound found in the skin of grapes possesses anti-inflammatory properties and can reduce cholesterol and prevent cancer. Wine also keeps the blood from thickening in the blood vessels —preventing blood clots, stroke, and plaque buildup. A little wine goes a long way, however: only one glass a day is necessary to provide benefits. If you drink more than a glass a day, the harm may outweigh the good. So drink up —but just a little." [10]

Exercise

You won't need the Captains to explain why this is important. We would only like to remind you that every little bit of exercise you can fit into the day is beneficial. Taking the stairs, parking far from the front door, or two minutes of "knee-high walking in place" while waiting for the kettle to boil are all exercise moments to take advantage of, especially for those of you with children, bosses, and deadlines crawling all over you. Every little bit helps.

We like incorporating a bit of Yoga into the daily grind. Stand in mountain or tree pose while brushing teeth, washing hands, standing in line, stirring the vegetables, cleaning dishes, etc. Drop into lotus pose a few times a day for a mini session, even if it's only for five minutes at a time. Once you start trying to fit Yoga into your established routine, you will notice all sorts of opportunities to get in a minute here and there.

Of course we recommend taking the time for a full work-out, yoga class, or run, but we can't always accomplish the full meal deal. Grabbing small exercise moments here and there can make a big impact on your physical well-being over time. And the more often you are in the "exercise mindset," the more you will be inspired to exercise.

Stress Level

It seems like a simple number system would work best here, but colors and symbols could be good, too. From the Old World, and the venerable William Wordsworth, a few thoughts on stress:

> The world is too much with us; late and soon,
> Getting and spending we lay waste our powers:
> Little we see in nature that is ours;
> We have given our hearts away, a sordid boon!
> The sea that bares her bosom to the moon;
> The winds that will be howling at all hours,
> And are up-gathered now like sleeping flowers;
> For this, for everything, we are out of tune;
> It moves us not. Great God! I'd rather be

A pagan suckled in a creed outworn;
So might I, standing on this pleasant lea,
Have glimpses that would make me less forlorn;
Have sight of Proteus rising from the sea;
Or hear old Triton blow his wreathe'd horn. [11]

Medication

Always take medications as directed by your doctor or practitioner. We would only like to add to this a lesser known quote from Hippocrates, the Father of Medicine: "A physician without a knowledge of Astrology has no right to call himself a physician."

Food Diary

This is a large topic about which volumes have been written. We encourage you to do as much research on healthy eating as you can find the time for. Your food is your fuel, so choose well. And since you truly are a result of what you eat, don't be fast, cheap, or unhealthy. Use the lines in this section to log all the food you eat during the day. Organize this space in a way that suits you best. We offer these suggestions: draw a vertical line in the middle of the space, using the left side for food consumed in the AM and the right side for food consumed in the PM. Another idea is to draw several vertical lines through the space and log your food intake according to proteins, vegetables, healthy fats, carbs, and fruit. There is no wrong way to log this data. Play around, change it up, and make it your own.

Notes & Curiosities

You determine how to use this space. If you want to expound on one of the topics, this would be a great place to do it. Or if you have a personal variable that you need to track, stick it in the notes section. We like using this space for grocery lists, "to do" lists, and doctor's appointments. We also like seeing this space used for conclusions of the day or notes about emerging patterns. You are the Captain ~ You decide.

Additional Notes

As previously mentioned, the HMS Log Book makes its port of call on the eastern seaboard of North America. For this reason, all moon phases and transits are listed according to Eastern Standard Time. Since many of you are using the journal abroad, we wish to bring this small detail to your attention as you may find that your New Moon, for example is happening on a different day than the journal portends. This happens when we try and stick a circular system onto a square calendar.

If you are finding that this oddity is disrupting your flow and you want to be more accurately informed of the celestial movements as they are witnessed in your particular location, we invite you to investigate an Ephemeris. When the captains of days gone by were scanning the skies for a fixed star to plot their course by, it was the ephemeris that told them where to look. This chart will inform you of the exact transits of all the planets, moon & sun, and can be readily found in your app store and online.

★ ★ ★ ★ ★

We also invite you to join the collective HMS crew online and with social media, if this resonates with you. If you have any questions about the journal, you will probably find the answers in Jen's YouTube videos and tutorials, along with barrels of life hacks, ideas and wisdom to help you on your self-awareness journey. Also check out Jen's blog posts on the official HMS Log Book website, www. hmslogbook.com and on Instagram, @hms.logbook. Here you'll find opportunities to learn about current cosmic energies, New Moon rituals, auric cleansing, vocal toning and so much more. You'll also stay up to date on Jen's workshop schedule and her favorite topic, reclaiming sovereignty. In her own words, "This is the most important inner work I have ever done, and sharing this concept is everything." Stay tuned for more opportunities to:

Reclaim Your Sovereignty

Part Three

The HMS Energy Wheel

"The predominant thought or the mental attitude is the magnet, and the law is that like attracts like. Consequently, the mental attitude will invariably attract such conditions as to correspond to its nature."
- Charles Haanel

We have been powerfully impacted by this concept of Haanel's, and many a late night at the Captain's Circle have we spent perusing its implications. We love the notion that we are indeed the Master of our destiny, and this has led us to the conclusion that there is an obvious need for more awareness of our "energy output."

To that end, The Captains are very proud to unveil The HMS Energy Wheel, which is a concept completely unique to the Log Book. The Energy Wheel is a process wherein you identify the quality of the energy you are radiating in each area of your life. Every day, every minute, every nanosecond, you transmit energy, whether you are aware of it or not. You do it consciously and sub-consciously. Why not bring full awareness to the energy that you naturally generate so that you can get to work on matching the frequency of the reality you want to live?

We are so often unaware that we are holding onto a negative frequency in a particular realm of our lives and that this serves as a beacon for attracting that same negative energy. The Captains invite you to sit with the Energy Wheel every New Moon, and describe the quality of the energy you hold for each area of your life. It is best to use one or two adjectives here, but this is your voyage, so please set the course that is best for you. Be honest and keep to The Code. On the next page you will find listed the twelve realms of the wheel, and sample questions to help you arrive at your answers. Awareness is the key to freedom -Take the wheel, Captain, and sail away.

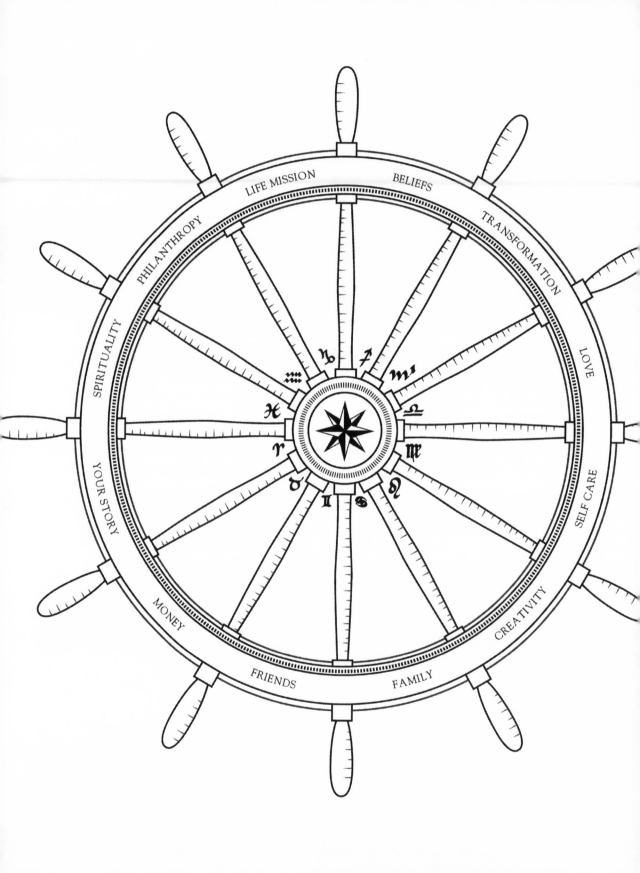

The HMS Energy Wheel & The Twelve Realms

- YOUR STORY
  This realm has to do with your self image, projected image, defense mechanisms, appearance, and your outlook on life. **Ask this question:** *How do I feel about myself?*

- MONEY
  This realm has to do with money and material possessions. **Ask the question:** *How do I feel about money?*

- FRIENDS
  This realm has to do with your friendly acquaintances. **Ask the questions:** *How do my friends make me feel?*

- FAMILY
  This realm has to do with psychological foundations and roots, family, home life. **Ask the question:** *How does my family and my home make me feel?*

- CREATIVITY
  This realm has to do with creative self-expression, pleasure and entertainment, all forms of play. **Ask the question:** *How do I feel about my creative self expression?*

- SELF-CARE
  This realm has to do with self-improvement, health, nutrition, your attitude towards food. **Ask the question:** *How do I feel about my body, mind & spirit?*

- ROMANTIC LOVE
  This realm has to do with companionship, marriage, and the "significant other." **Ask the question:** *How do I feel about love?*

- TRANSFORMATION
  This realm has to do with transformation and crisis, our attitude towards crisis and change, & personal growth and transformation. **Ask the question:** *How do I feel about change?*

- BELIEF SYSTEM
  This realm has to do with our personal belief system, our sense of adventure, exploration, religious beliefs and personal philosophy, & higher education. **Ask the question:** *How do I feel about my belief system?*

- LIFE MISSION
  This realm has to do with career and profession, contribution to society, position in society, social standing, & reputation. **Ask the question:** *How do I feel about my life mission?*

- PHILANTHROPY
  This realm has to do with giving, organizations, hopes, wishes, & humanity. **Ask the question:** *How do I feel about giving?*

- SPIRITUALITY
  This realm has to do with soul growth, that which is hidden or below the surface, karma, self-undoing, hidden strengths and hidden weaknesses, & dreams. **Ask the question:** *How do I feel about spirituality?*

New Moon Intentions

Now that you are acquainted with the HMS Energy Wheel and feeling good about how to identify your energy output, it's time to incorporate this knowledge into your New Moon Intention practice. The new moon is a very special phase in the lunar cycle, and many beautiful traditions have formed over the centuries to celebrate this magical time. As this phase supports the energy of beginnings and initiation, the captains especially like the idea of hand writing ten intentions within the first 24 hours after the new moon is birthed. Consult an ephemeris to determine what time this aspect occurs in your time zone, then write your intentions soon after to be sure and capture that new moon juiciness. It's best to create some quiet space for this monthly exercise. Begin by lighting a candle, practicing some deep breathing to get yourself centered, and maybe listening to some lovely 432 Hz music to set a relaxing mood. Anything you can do to raise your vibration first will amplify the benefit of this process.

One bit of advice is to be sure to phrase your intentions in the affirmative tense, such as "I am grateful for all the abundance and love in my life." The Log Book gives you a heads up the day before each new moon, and lists the themes around which to center your intentions. When the moon is in Libra, for example, it would be most effective to focus on concepts such as improving existing relationships, enhancing social skills, attracting a suitable life partner, and amplifying self-confidence. This is because we are absorbing the energy of Libra through the lens of the new moon, which spotlights the dominant themes in that astrological sign. And loosely translated, this means, the energy of the Libra new moon will support intentions framed around relationships and love. Refer back to page 17 for a deeper dive into the intention setting ritual as well as some important tips and tools.

Give it a whirl, and see what you think. Intentions are super powerful, especially when spoken out loud. As we move closer towards the Age of Aquarius, many of us are coming into a deeper knowing of our innate manifesting power. Inspiration is landing in practical ways whereas before the words may have just hung about in the conceptual realm. Wayne Dyer reminds us that we must believe it to see it, and Andrew Bartzis tells us we must name it to claim it. These transformational ideas have deeply inspired our intention setting practice, and we are delighted to support this awakening with a new feature in the journal. The HMS Log Book has been upgraded to include space to write your new moon intentions each month, and we encourage you to fill this space with every detail imaginable. When placing your order with the Youniverse, it's wise to do so with as much clarity and precision as possible.

The Grand Cycle of Life

Cancer

June 21 - July 22

ELEMENT: WATER

QUALITY: CARDINAL

RULING PLANET: THE MOON

CONSTELLATION: THE CRAB

MODE: FEELING

MOTTO: "I FEEL"

IN THE GRAND CYCLE OF LIFE: 21-28 YEARS

THEMES:
PERSONAL EMOTIONS, THE SUBCONSCIOUS,
DREAMS, CRUSTACEAN ARMOR, HIDING,
FAMILY & THE HOME, FERTILITY

ELEMENT			SEASON

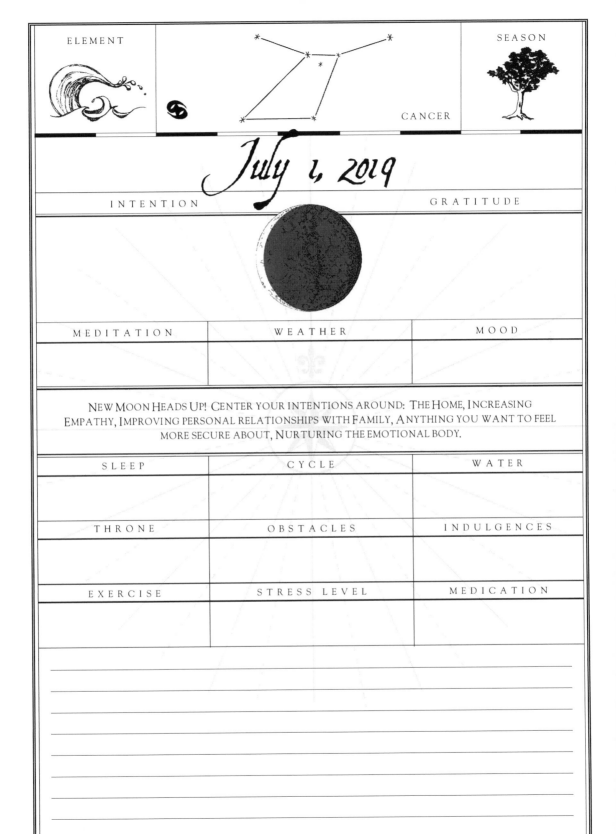

CANCER

July 1, 2019

INTENTION		GRATITUDE

MEDITATION	WEATHER	MOOD

NEW MOON HEADS UP! CENTER YOUR INTENTIONS AROUND: THE HOME, INCREASING EMPATHY, IMPROVING PERSONAL RELATIONSHIPS WITH FAMILY, ANYTHING YOU WANT TO FEEL MORE SECURE ABOUT, NURTURING THE EMOTIONAL BODY.

SLEEP	CYCLE	WATER
THRONE	OBSTACLES	INDULGENCES
EXERCISE	STRESS LEVEL	MEDICATION

The HMS Energy Wheel

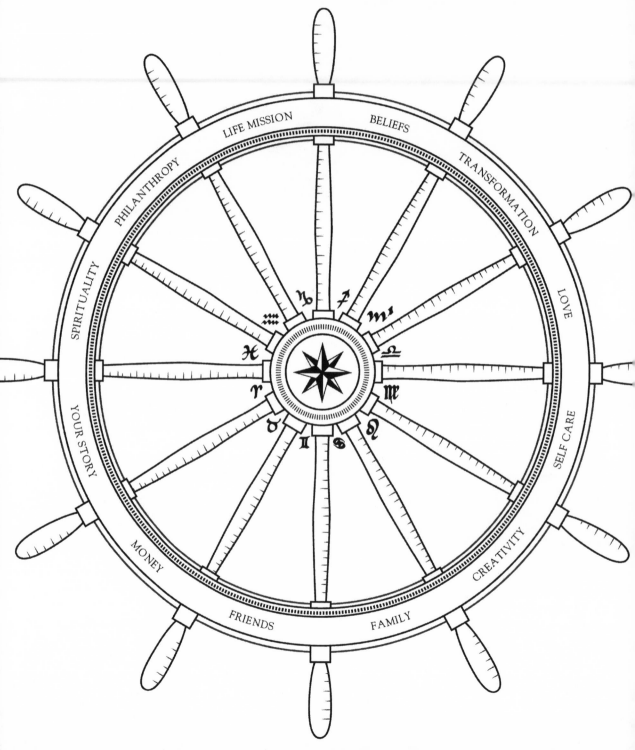

New Moon Intentions

3:16PM EST

New Moon Intentions

3:16PM EST

ELEMENT		CANCER	SEASON

July 2, 2019

INTENTION	GRATITUDE

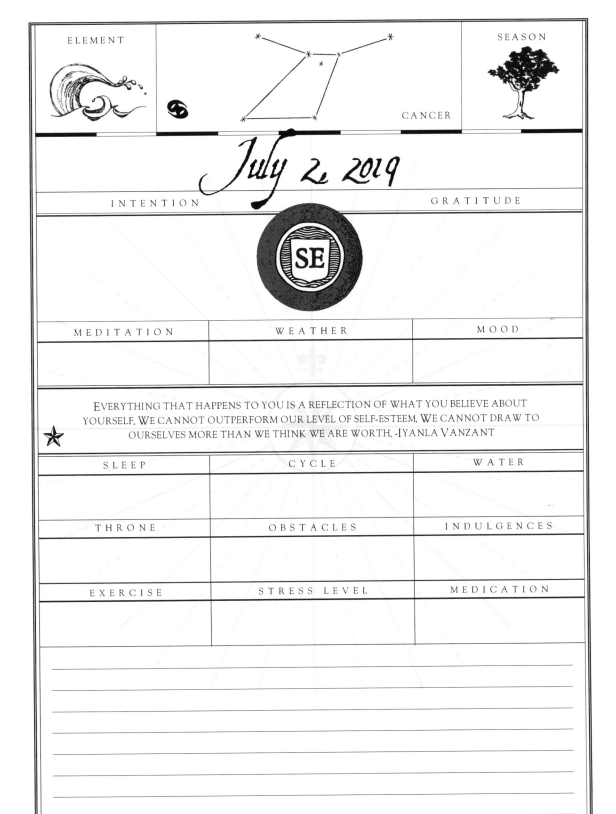

MEDITATION	WEATHER	MOOD

EVERYTHING THAT HAPPENS TO YOU IS A REFLECTION OF WHAT YOU BELIEVE ABOUT YOURSELF. WE CANNOT OUTPERFORM OUR LEVEL OF SELF-ESTEEM. WE CANNOT DRAW TO OURSELVES MORE THAN WE THINK WE ARE WORTH. -IYANLA VANZANT

SLEEP	CYCLE	WATER
THRONE	OBSTACLES	INDULGENCES
EXERCISE	STRESS LEVEL	MEDICATION

ELEMENT			SEASON

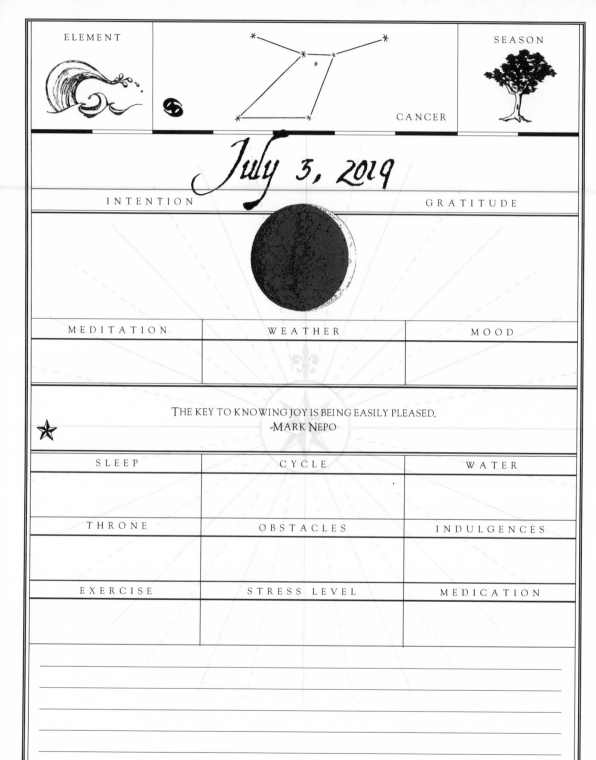

CANCER

July 3, 2019

INTENTION		GRATITUDE

MEDITATION	WEATHER	MOOD

THE KEY TO KNOWING JOY IS BEING EASILY PLEASED.
-MARK NEPO

SLEEP	CYCLE	WATER
THRONE	OBSTACLES	INDULGENCES
EXERCISE	STRESS LEVEL	MEDICATION

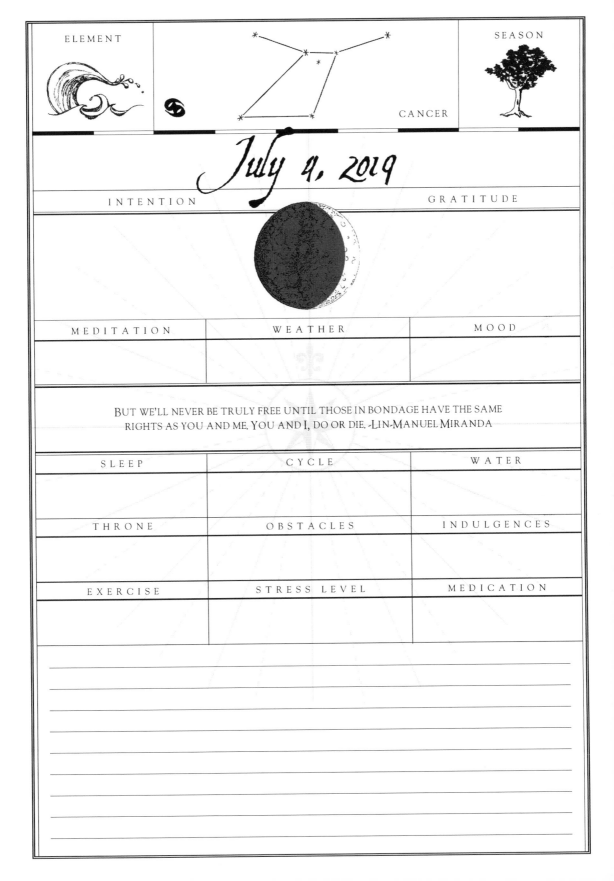

ELEMENT			SEASON

CANCER

July 4, 2019

INTENTION		GRATITUDE

MEDITATION	WEATHER	MOOD

BUT WE'LL NEVER BE TRULY FREE UNTIL THOSE IN BONDAGE HAVE THE SAME
RIGHTS AS YOU AND ME. YOU AND I, DO OR DIE. -LIN-MANUEL MIRANDA

SLEEP	CYCLE	WATER
THRONE	OBSTACLES	INDULGENCES
EXERCISE	STRESS LEVEL	MEDICATION

ELEMENT		CANCER	SEASON

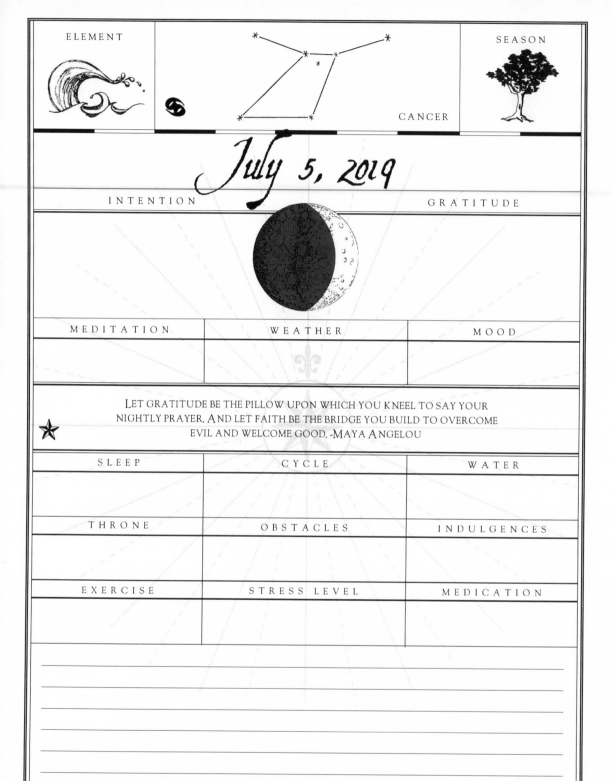

July 5, 2019

INTENTION		GRATITUDE

MEDITATION	WEATHER	MOOD

LET GRATITUDE BE THE PILLOW UPON WHICH YOU KNEEL TO SAY YOUR
NIGHTLY PRAYER. AND LET FAITH BE THE BRIDGE YOU BUILD TO OVERCOME
EVIL AND WELCOME GOOD. -MAYA ANGELOU

SLEEP	CYCLE	WATER
THRONE	OBSTACLES	INDULGENCES
EXERCISE	STRESS LEVEL	MEDICATION

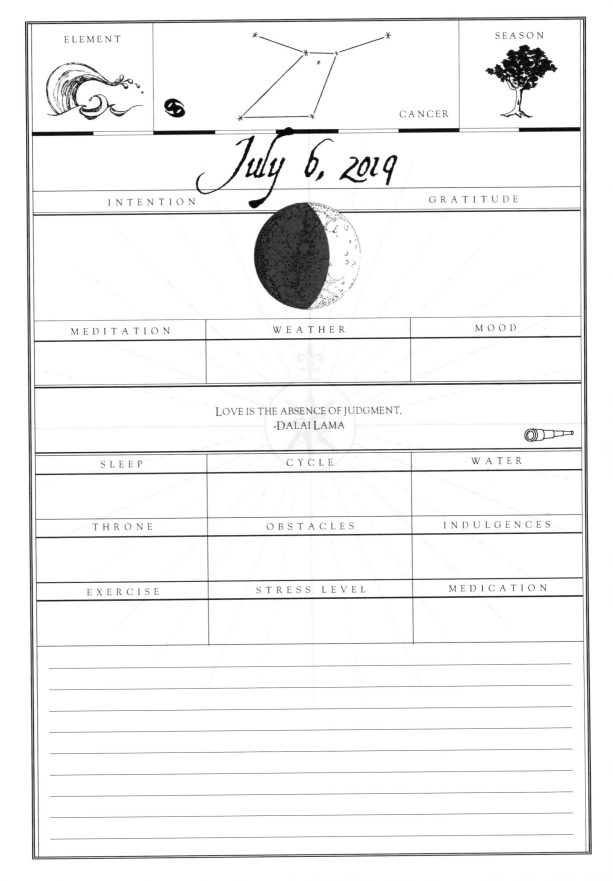

ELEMENT

SEASON

CANCER

July 6, 2019

INTENTION

GRATITUDE

MEDITATION

WEATHER

MOOD

LOVE IS THE ABSENCE OF JUDGMENT.
-DALAI LAMA

SLEEP

CYCLE

WATER

THRONE

OBSTACLES

INDULGENCES

EXERCISE

STRESS LEVEL

MEDICATION

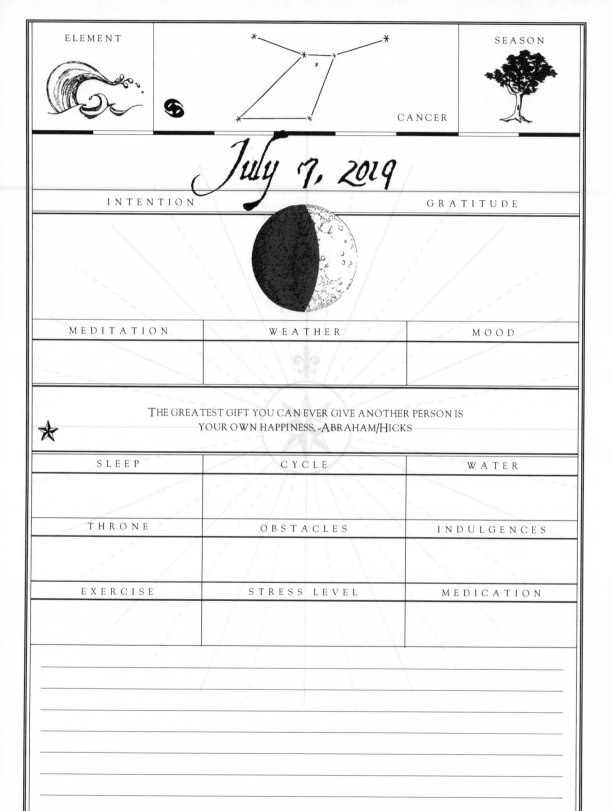

ELEMENT

CANCER

SEASON

July 7, 2019

INTENTION   GRATITUDE

MEDITATION	WEATHER	MOOD

THE GREATEST GIFT YOU CAN EVER GIVE ANOTHER PERSON IS
YOUR OWN HAPPINESS. -ABRAHAM/HICKS

SLEEP	CYCLE	WATER
THRONE	OBSTACLES	INDULGENCES
EXERCISE	STRESS LEVEL	MEDICATION

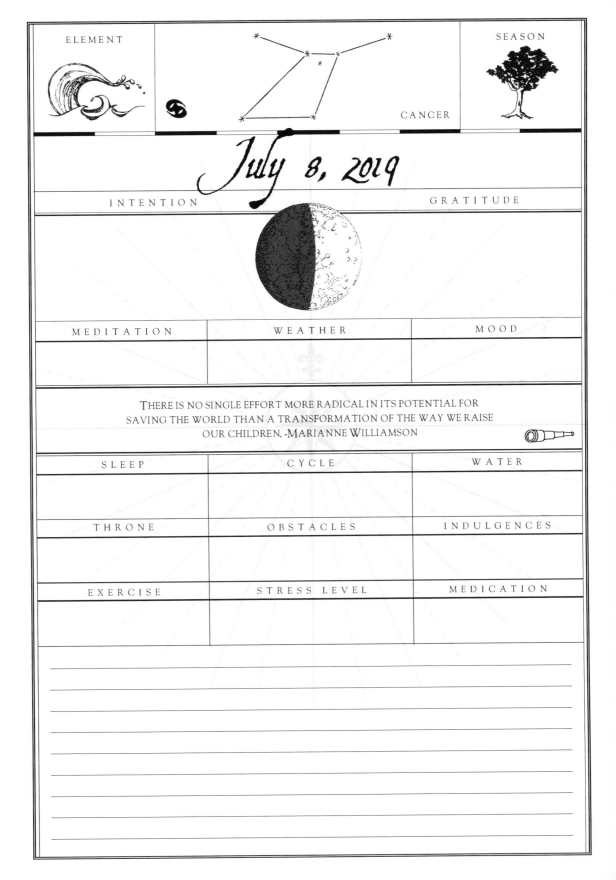

ELEMENT

SEASON

CANCER

July 8, 2019

INTENTION

GRATITUDE

MEDITATION | WEATHER | MOOD

THERE IS NO SINGLE EFFORT MORE RADICAL IN ITS POTENTIAL FOR
SAVING THE WORLD THAN A TRANSFORMATION OF THE WAY WE RAISE
OUR CHILDREN. -MARIANNE WILLIAMSON

SLEEP | CYCLE | WATER

THRONE | OBSTACLES | INDULGENCES

EXERCISE | STRESS LEVEL | MEDICATION

ELEMENT		CANCER	SEASON

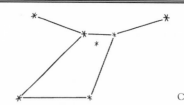

July 9, 2019

INTENTION	GRATITUDE

MEDITATION	WEATHER	MOOD

ACHIEVING THE IMPOSSIBLE REQUIRES THAT YOU OUTWIT YOUR VOICE OF REASON
AND ACCESS THE WHIMSICAL PART OF YOUR NATURE THAT INHERENTLY DELIGHTS IN
THE POSSIBILITIES OF THE IMAGINATION. - CAROLINE MYSS

SLEEP	CYCLE	WATER
THRONE	OBSTACLES	INDULGENCES
EXERCISE	STRESS LEVEL	MEDICATION

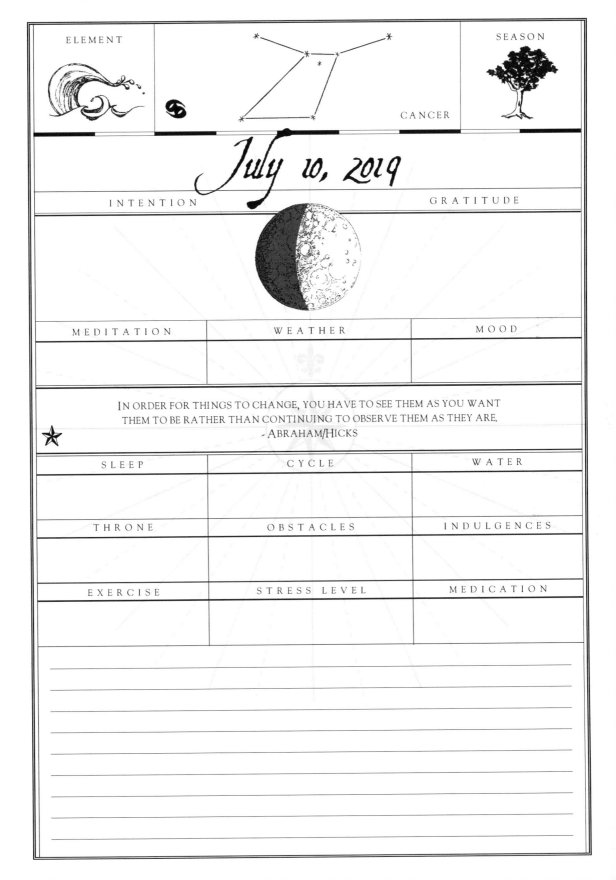

ELEMENT

SEASON

CANCER

July 10, 2019

INTENTION   GRATITUDE

MEDITATION   WEATHER   MOOD

IN ORDER FOR THINGS TO CHANGE, YOU HAVE TO SEE THEM AS YOU WANT
THEM TO BE RATHER THAN CONTINUING TO OBSERVE THEM AS THEY ARE.
- ABRAHAM/HICKS

SLEEP   CYCLE   WATER

THRONE   OBSTACLES   INDULGENCES

EXERCISE   STRESS LEVEL   MEDICATION

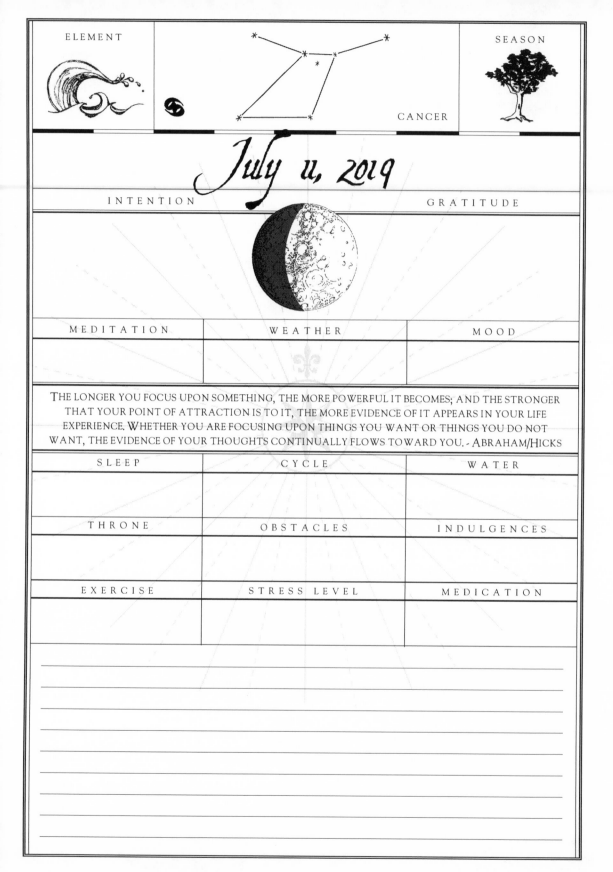

ELEMENT		CANCER	SEASON

July 11, 2019

INTENTION		GRATITUDE

MEDITATION	WEATHER	MOOD

THE LONGER YOU FOCUS UPON SOMETHING, THE MORE POWERFUL IT BECOMES; AND THE STRONGER THAT YOUR POINT OF ATTRACTION IS TO IT, THE MORE EVIDENCE OF IT APPEARS IN YOUR LIFE EXPERIENCE. WHETHER YOU ARE FOCUSING UPON THINGS YOU WANT OR THINGS YOU DO NOT WANT, THE EVIDENCE OF YOUR THOUGHTS CONTINUALLY FLOWS TOWARD YOU. - ABRAHAM/HICKS

SLEEP	CYCLE	WATER
THRONE	OBSTACLES	INDULGENCES
EXERCISE	STRESS LEVEL	MEDICATION

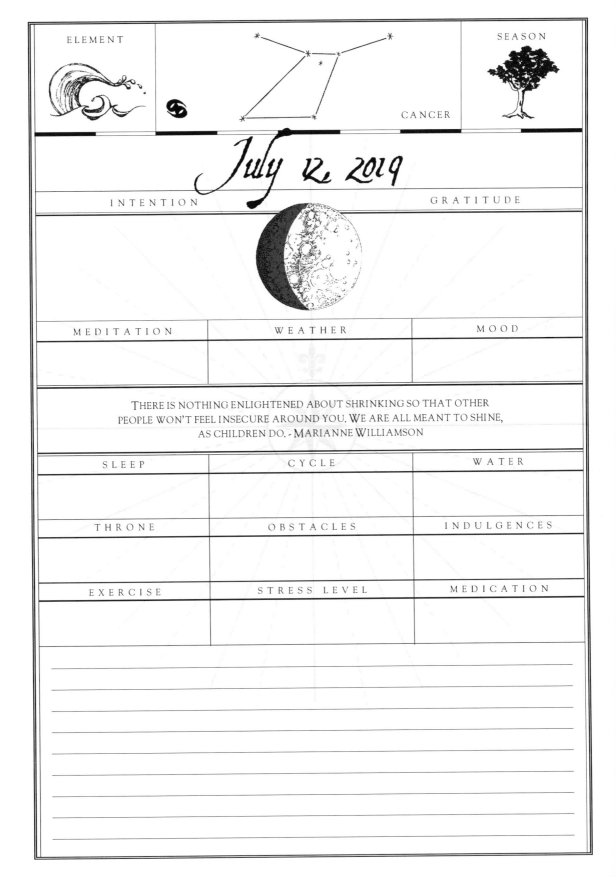

ELEMENT

SEASON

CANCER

July 12, 2019

INTENTION

GRATITUDE

MEDITATION | WEATHER | MOOD

THERE IS NOTHING ENLIGHTENED ABOUT SHRINKING SO THAT OTHER
PEOPLE WON'T FEEL INSECURE AROUND YOU. WE ARE ALL MEANT TO SHINE,
AS CHILDREN DO. - MARIANNE WILLIAMSON

SLEEP | CYCLE | WATER

THRONE | OBSTACLES | INDULGENCES

EXERCISE | STRESS LEVEL | MEDICATION

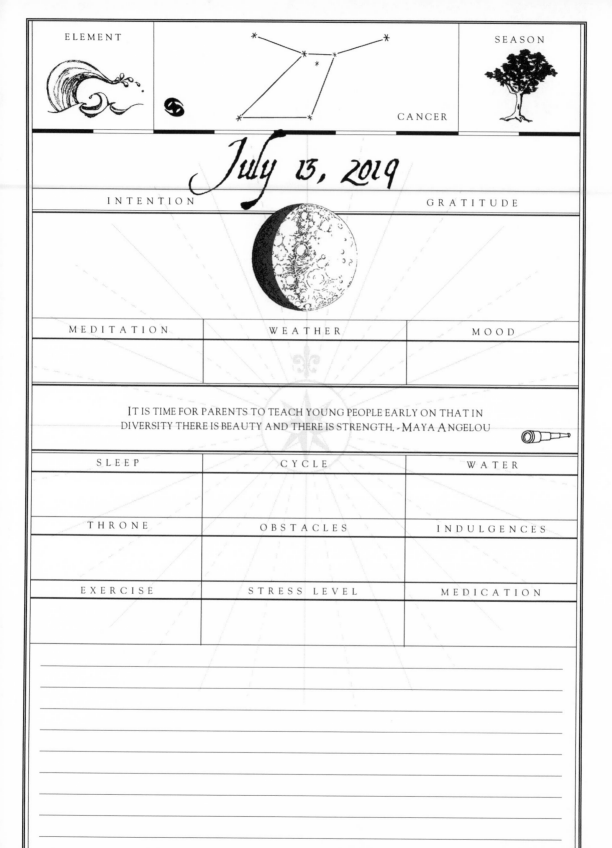

ELEMENT

SEASON

CANCER

July 13, 2019

INTENTION

GRATITUDE

MEDITATION	WEATHER	MOOD

IT IS TIME FOR PARENTS TO TEACH YOUNG PEOPLE EARLY ON THAT IN
DIVERSITY THERE IS BEAUTY AND THERE IS STRENGTH. - MAYA ANGELOU

SLEEP	CYCLE	WATER
THRONE	OBSTACLES	INDULGENCES
EXERCISE	STRESS LEVEL	MEDICATION

July 14, 2019

INTENTION		GRATITUDE

MEDITATION	WEATHER	MOOD

WHATEVER THE PROBLEM, BE PART OF THE SOLUTION. DON'T JUST SIT
AROUND RAISING QUESTIONS AND POINTING OUT OBSTACLES. -TINA FEY

SLEEP	CYCLE	WATER
THRONE	OBSTACLES	INDULGENCES
EXERCISE	STRESS LEVEL	MEDICATION

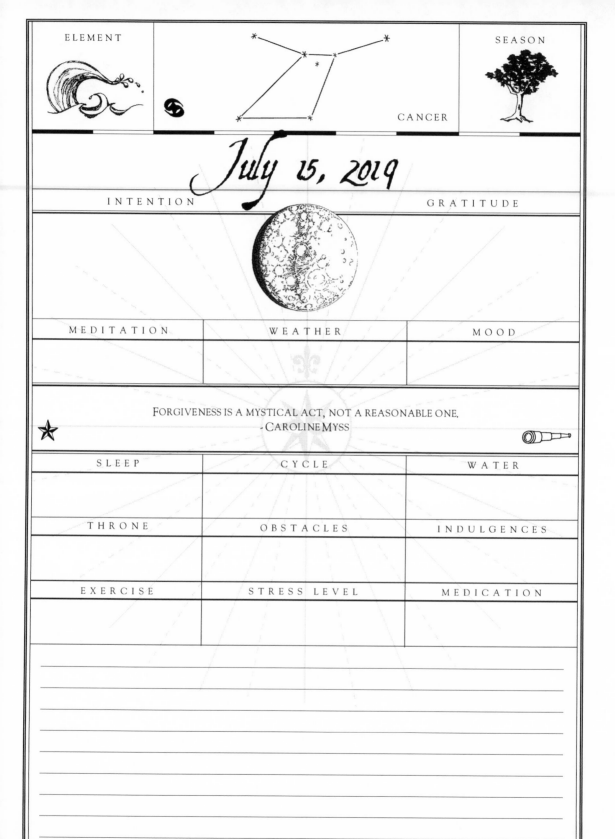

ELEMENT

SEASON

CANCER

July 15, 2019

INTENTION	GRATITUDE

MEDITATION	WEATHER	MOOD

FORGIVENESS IS A MYSTICAL ACT, NOT A REASONABLE ONE.
- CAROLINE MYSS

SLEEP	CYCLE	WATER
THRONE	OBSTACLES	INDULGENCES
EXERCISE	STRESS LEVEL	MEDICATION

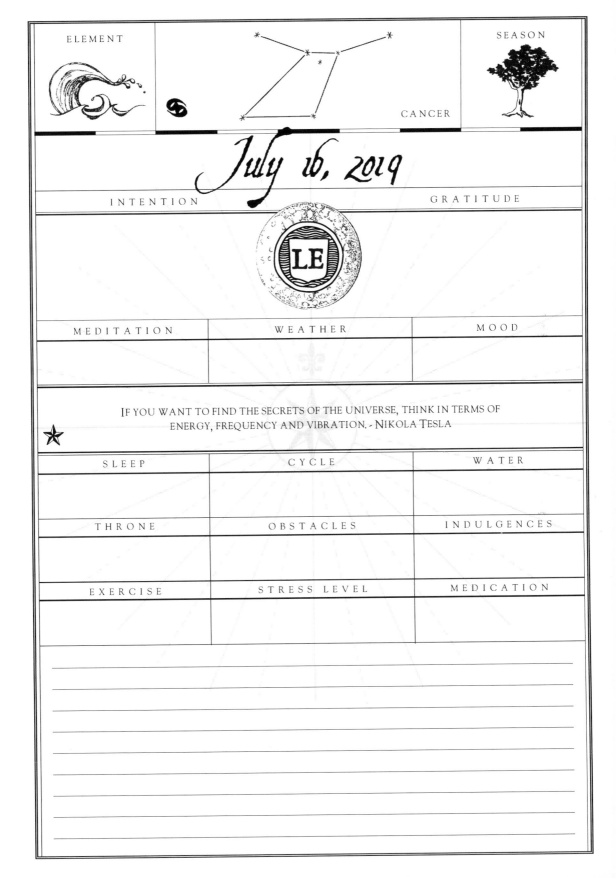

ELEMENT			SEASON

CANCER

July 16, 2019

INTENTION	GRATITUDE

MEDITATION	WEATHER	MOOD

IF YOU WANT TO FIND THE SECRETS OF THE UNIVERSE, THINK IN TERMS OF
ENERGY, FREQUENCY AND VIBRATION. - NIKOLA TESLA

SLEEP	CYCLE	WATER
THRONE	OBSTACLES	INDULGENCES
EXERCISE	STRESS LEVEL	MEDICATION

CANCER

July 17, 2019

INTENTION		GRATITUDE

MEDITATION	WEATHER	MOOD

LOOK AROUND LESS, IMAGINE MORE.
- ABRAHAM/HICKS

SLEEP	CYCLE	WATER

THRONE	OBSTACLES	INDULGENCES

EXERCISE	STRESS LEVEL	MEDICATION

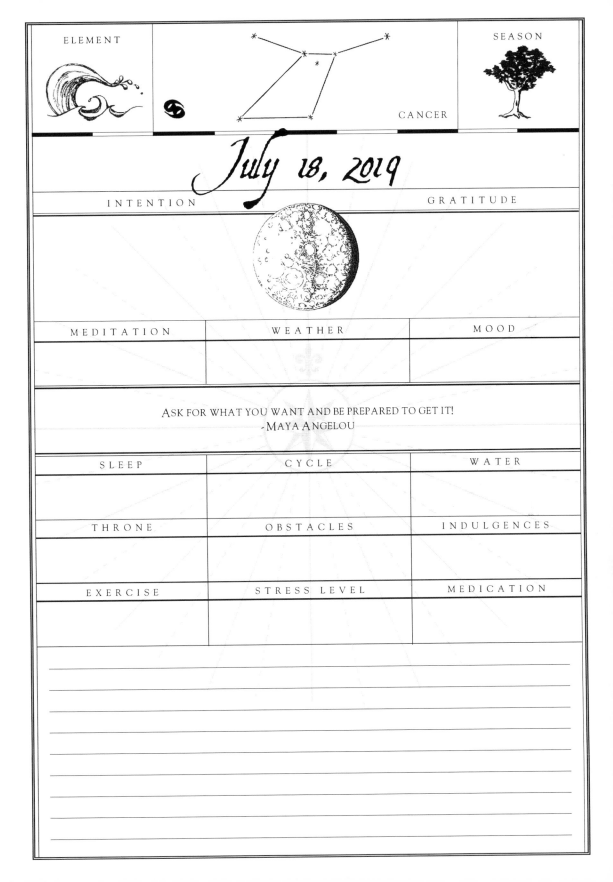

ELEMENT		CANCER	SEASON

July 18, 2019

INTENTION		GRATITUDE

MEDITATION	WEATHER	MOOD

ASK FOR WHAT YOU WANT AND BE PREPARED TO GET IT!
-MAYA ANGELOU

SLEEP	CYCLE	WATER

THRONE	OBSTACLES	INDULGENCES

EXERCISE	STRESS LEVEL	MEDICATION

July 19, 2019

INTENTION	GRATITUDE

MEDITATION	WEATHER	MOOD

OUR DEEPEST FEAR IS NOT THAT WE ARE INADEQUATE. OUR DEEPEST FEAR IS THAT WE ARE POWERFUL BEYOND MEASURE. IT IS OUR LIGHT, NOT OUR DARKNESS THAT MOST FRIGHTENS US. - MARIANNE WILLIAMSON

SLEEP	CYCLE	WATER

THRONE	OBSTACLES	INDULGENCES

EXERCISE	STRESS LEVEL	MEDICATION

ELEMENT			SEASON
		CANCER	

July 20, 2019

INTENTION		GRATITUDE

MEDITATION	WEATHER	MOOD

EMOTIONS ARE LIKE PASSING STORMS, AND YOU HAVE TO REMIND YOURSELF THAT IT WON'T RAIN FOREVER. YOU JUST HAVE TO SIT DOWN AND WATCH IT POUR OUTSIDE AND THEN PEEK YOUR HEAD OUT WHEN IT LOOKS DRY. - AMY POEHLER

SLEEP	CYCLE	WATER
THRONE	OBSTACLES	INDULGENCES
EXERCISE	STRESS LEVEL	MEDICATION

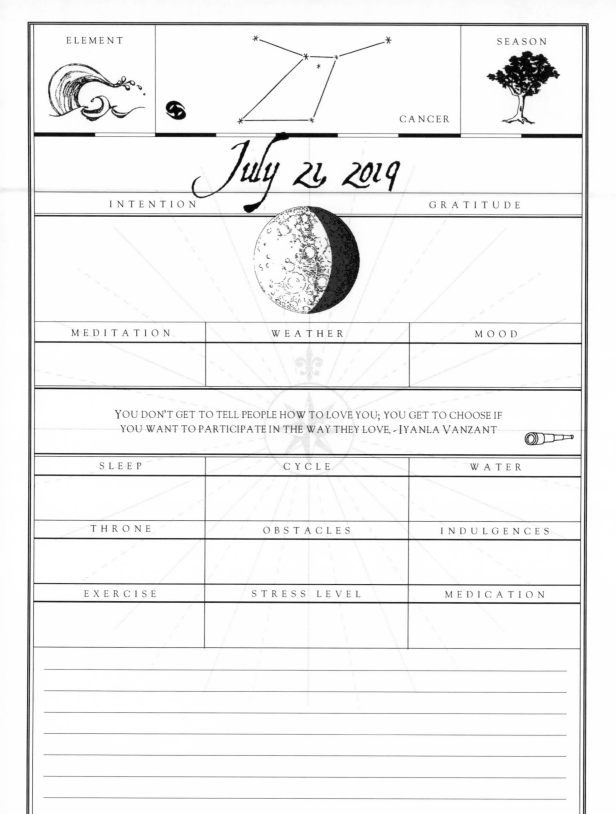

ELEMENT

SEASON

CANCER

July 21 2019

INTENTION

GRATITUDE

MEDITATION	WEATHER	MOOD

YOU DON'T GET TO TELL PEOPLE HOW TO LOVE YOU; YOU GET TO CHOOSE IF
YOU WANT TO PARTICIPATE IN THE WAY THEY LOVE. ~ IYANLA VANZANT

SLEEP	CYCLE	WATER
THRONE	OBSTACLES	INDULGENCES
EXERCISE	STRESS LEVEL	MEDICATION

ELEMENT		CANCER	SEASON

July 22, 2019

INTENTION		GRATITUDE

MEDITATION	WEATHER	MOOD

IF YOU WANT IT AND EXPECT IT, IT WILL BE YOURS VERY SOON.
- ABRAHAM/HICKS

SLEEP	CYCLE	WATER
THRONE	OBSTACLES	INDULGENCES
EXERCISE	STRESS LEVEL	MEDICATION

Leo

July 23 – August 23

ELEMENT: FIRE

QUALITY: FIXED

RULING PLANET: THE SUN

CONSTELLATION: THE LION

MODE: INTUITION

MOTTO: "I CREATE"

IN THE GRAND CYCLE OF LIFE: 28-35 YEARS

THEMES:
AMBITION, POWER, SELF-CONFIDENCE,
COURAGE, CREATIVITY, ENJOYMENT, PASSION, PLAY,
FEROCITY, INSPIRATION, DRAMA

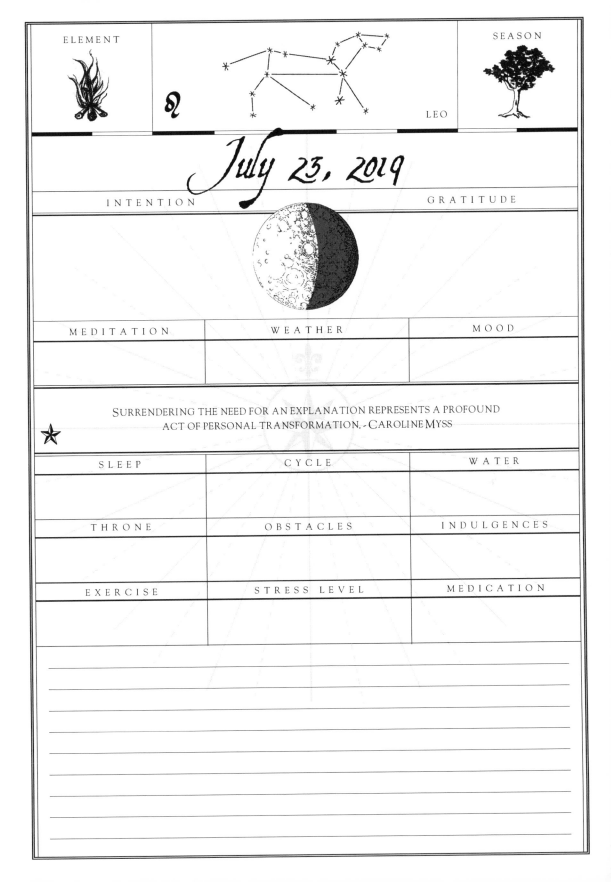

ELEMENT

SEASON

♌

LEO

July 23, 2019

INTENTION

GRATITUDE

MEDITATION

WEATHER

MOOD

SURRENDERING THE NEED FOR AN EXPLANATION REPRESENTS A PROFOUND
ACT OF PERSONAL TRANSFORMATION. - CAROLINE MYSS

SLEEP

CYCLE

WATER

THRONE

OBSTACLES

INDULGENCES

EXERCISE

STRESS LEVEL

MEDICATION

ELEMENT		SEASON
♌	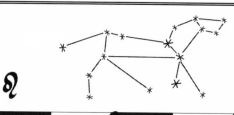 LEO	

July 29, 2019

INTENTION		GRATITUDE

MEDITATION	WEATHER	MOOD

COMPARISON IS AN ACT OF VIOLENCE AGAINST THE SELF.
- IYANLA VANZANT

SLEEP	CYCLE	WATER

THRONE	OBSTACLES	INDULGENCES

EXERCISE	STRESS LEVEL	MEDICATION

ELEMENT				SEASON
	♌		LEO	

July 25, 2019

INTENTION	GRATITUDE

MEDITATION	WEATHER	MOOD

IF SOMETHING YOU WANT IS SLOW TO COME TO YOU, IT CAN BE FOR ONLY ONE
REASON: YOU ARE SPENDING MORE TIME FOCUSED UPON ITS ABSENCE THAN
YOU ARE ABOUT ITS PRESENCE. - ABRAHAM/HICKS

SLEEP	CYCLE	WATER
THRONE	OBSTACLES	INDULGENCES
EXERCISE	STRESS LEVEL	MEDICATION

July 26, 2019

INTENTION	GRATITUDE

MEDITATION	WEATHER	MOOD

JUST LET GO. LET GO OF HOW YOU THOUGHT YOUR LIFE SHOULD BE,
AND EMBRACE THE LIFE THAT IS TRYING TO WORK ITS WAY INTO YOUR
CONSCIOUSNESS. - CAROLINE MYSS

SLEEP	CYCLE	WATER

THRONE	OBSTACLES	INDULGENCES

EXERCISE	STRESS LEVEL	MEDICATION

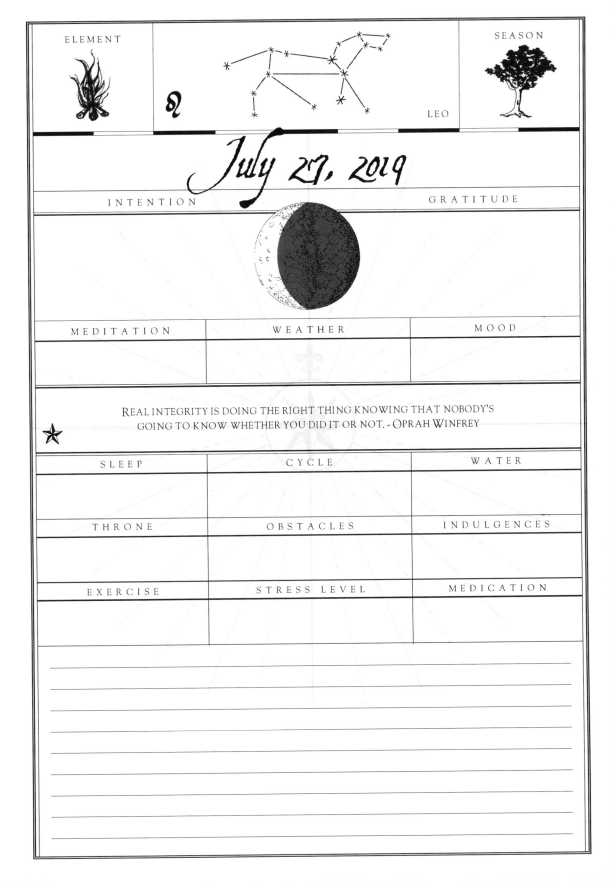

ELEMENT

SEASON

LEO

ॠ

July 27, 2019

INTENTION

GRATITUDE

MEDITATION

WEATHER

MOOD

REAL INTEGRITY IS DOING THE RIGHT THING KNOWING THAT NOBODY'S
GOING TO KNOW WHETHER YOU DID IT OR NOT. - OPRAH WINFREY

SLEEP	CYCLE	WATER
THRONE	OBSTACLES	INDULGENCES
EXERCISE	STRESS LEVEL	MEDICATION

July 28, 2019

INTENTION		GRATITUDE

MEDITATION	WEATHER	MOOD

WHEN YOU STAND AND SHARE YOUR STORY IN AN EMPOWERING WAY, YOUR STORY
WILL HEAL YOU AND YOUR STORY WILL HEAL SOMEBODY ELSE. - IYANLA VANZANT

SLEEP	CYCLE	WATER
THRONE	OBSTACLES	INDULGENCES
EXERCISE	STRESS LEVEL	MEDICATION

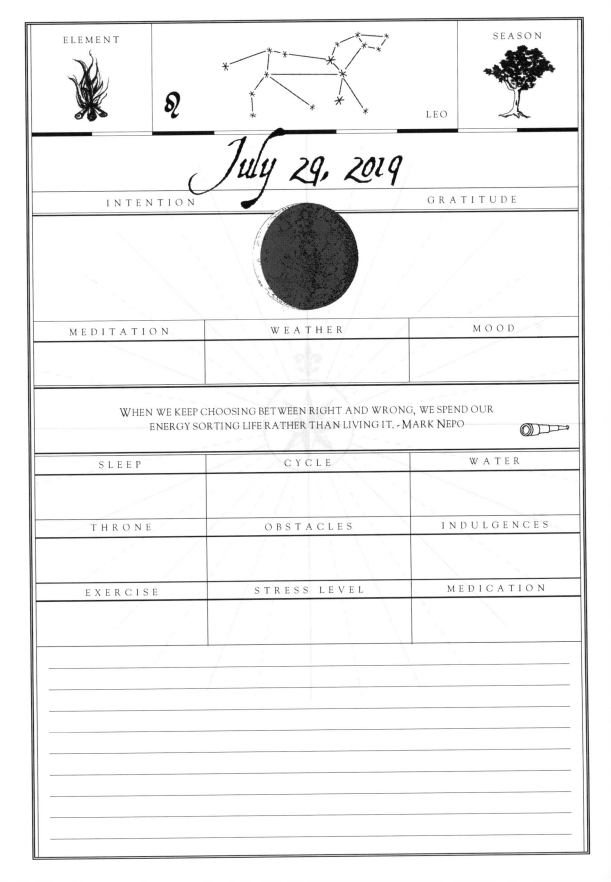

ELEMENT	♌			SEASON
			LEO	

July 29, 2019

INTENTION		GRATITUDE

MEDITATION	WEATHER	MOOD

WHEN WE KEEP CHOOSING BETWEEN RIGHT AND WRONG, WE SPEND OUR
ENERGY SORTING LIFE RATHER THAN LIVING IT. - MARK NEPO

SLEEP	CYCLE	WATER
THRONE	OBSTACLES	INDULGENCES
EXERCISE	STRESS LEVEL	MEDICATION

ELEMENT		LEO	SEASON
	♌		

July 30, 2019

INTENTION	GRATITUDE

MEDITATION	WEATHER	MOOD

NEW MOON HEADS UP! CENTER YOUR INTENTIONS AROUND: ACTIVATING YOUR ROMANTIC LIFE, STARTING A NEW CREATIVE PROJECT, MAKING MORE TIME FOR PLAY, INCREASING SELF-CONFIDENCE, IMPROVING YOUR RELATIONSHIP WITH YOUR CHILDREN OR YOUR INNER-CHILD.

SLEEP	CYCLE	WATER
THRONE	OBSTACLES	INDULGENCES
EXERCISE	STRESS LEVEL	MEDICATION

The HMS Energy Wheel

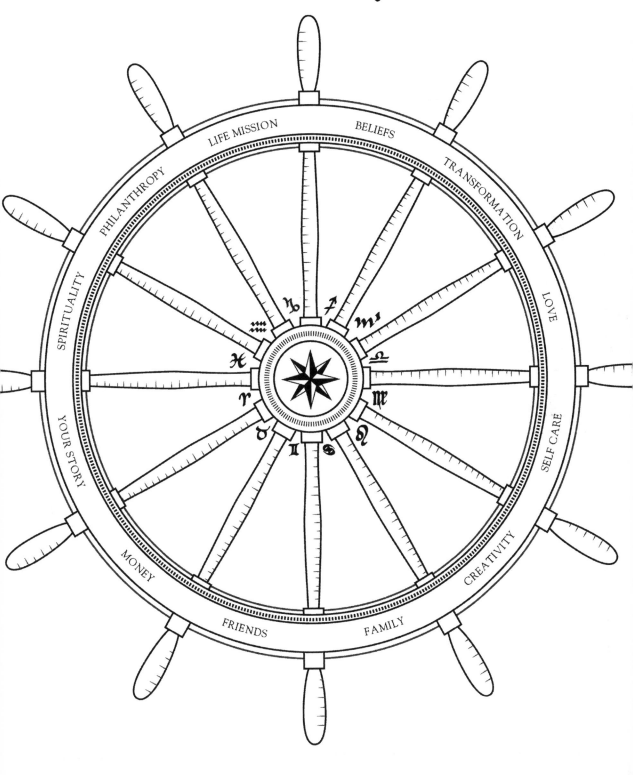

New Moon Intentions

New Moon Intentions

11:11PM EST

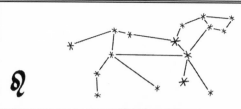
July 31, 2019

INTENTION   GRATITUDE

MEDITATION	WEATHER	MOOD

A PERSON'S TRAGEDY DOES NOT MAKE UP THEIR ENTIRE LIFE. A STORY CARVES DEEP GROOVES INTO OUR BRAINS EACH TIME WE TELL IT. BUT WE AREN'T ONE STORY. WE CAN CHANGE OUR STORIES. WE CAN WRITE OUR OWN. - AMY POEHLER

SLEEP	CYCLE	WATER
THRONE	OBSTACLES	INDULGENCES
EXERCISE	STRESS LEVEL	MEDICATION

August 1, 2019

INTENTION		GRATITUDE

MEDITATION	WEATHER	MOOD

REST SATISFIED WITH DOING WELL AND LEAVE OTHERS TO TALK OF
YOU AS THEY WILL. -PYTHAGORAS

SLEEP	CYCLE	WATER
THRONE	OBSTACLES	INDULGENCES
EXERCISE	STRESS LEVEL	MEDICATION

ELEMENT			SEASON

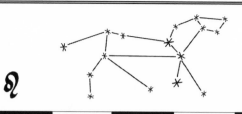

♌

LEO

August 2, 2019

INTENTION	GRATITUDE

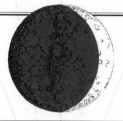

MEDITATION	WEATHER	MOOD

WHATEVER OPENS US IS NOT AS IMPORTANT AS WHAT IT OPENS.
-MARK NEPO

SLEEP	CYCLE	WATER
THRONE	OBSTACLES	INDULGENCES
EXERCISE	STRESS LEVEL	MEDICATION

_____
_____
_____
_____
_____
_____
_____
_____

ELEMENT			SEASON

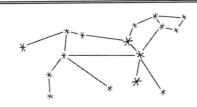

LEO

August 3, 2019

INTENTION		GRATITUDE

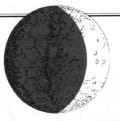

MEDITATION	WEATHER	MOOD

YOU ARE ACTUALLY PRE-PAVING YOUR FUTURE EXPERIENCES CONSTANTLY.
... YOU ARE CONTINUALLY PROJECTING YOUR EXPECTATIONS INTO YOUR
FUTURE EXPERIENCES. - ABRAHAM/HICKS

SLEEP	CYCLE	WATER
THRONE	OBSTACLES	INDULGENCES
EXERCISE	STRESS LEVEL	MEDICATION

ELEMENT			SEASON

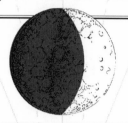

♌

LEO

August 9, 2019

INTENTION		GRATITUDE

MEDITATION	WEATHER	MOOD

WE CAN CONTROL OUR LIVES BY CONTROLLING OUR PERCEPTIONS.
- DR. BRUCE LIPTON

SLEEP	CYCLE	WATER
THRONE	OBSTACLES	INDULGENCES
EXERCISE	STRESS LEVEL	MEDICATION

ELEMENT		LEO	SEASON
	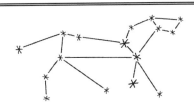		

August 5, 2019

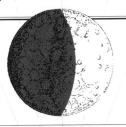

INTENTION		GRATITUDE

MEDITATION	WEATHER	MOOD

MOST PERSONS ARE SO ABSORBED IN THE CONTEMPLATION OF THE OUTSIDE WORLD THAT THEY ARE WHOLLY OBLIVIOUS TO WHAT IS PASSING ON WITHIN THEMSELVES. - NIKOLA TESLA

SLEEP	CYCLE	WATER
THRONE	OBSTACLES	INDULGENCES
EXERCISE	STRESS LEVEL	MEDICATION

ELEMENT		LEO	SEASON

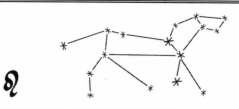

August 6, 2019

INTENTION		GRATITUDE

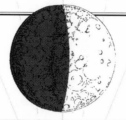

MEDITATION	WEATHER	MOOD

YOU DON'T BECOME WHAT YOU WANT, YOU BECOME WHAT YOU BELIEVE.
- OPRAH WINFREY

SLEEP	CYCLE	WATER
THRONE	OBSTACLES	INDULGENCES
EXERCISE	STRESS LEVEL	MEDICATION

ELEMENT				SEASON
	♌	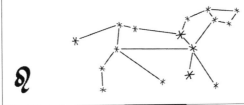	LEO	

August 7, 2019

INTENTION		GRATITUDE

MEDITATION	WEATHER	MOOD

JOY IS WHAT HAPPENS TO US WHEN WE ALLOW OURSELVES TO RECOGNIZE
HOW GOOD THINGS REALLY ARE. - MARIANNE WILLIAMSON

SLEEP	CYCLE	WATER
THRONE	OBSTACLES	INDULGENCES
EXERCISE	STRESS LEVEL	MEDICATION

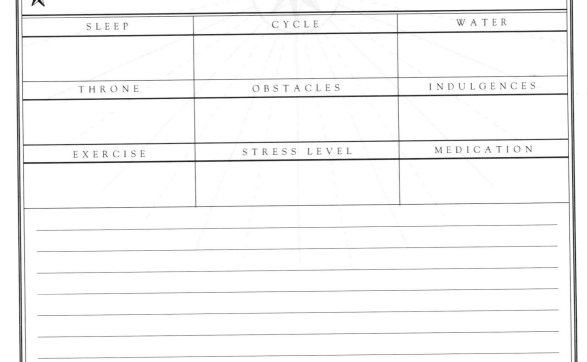

ELEMENT		SEASON

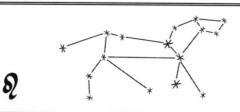

♌

LEO

August 8, 2019

INTENTION	GRATITUDE

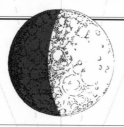

MEDITATION	WEATHER	MOOD

WHAT IS IT THAT WOULD MAKE A CREATURE AS FIERCE, MAJESTIC AND POWERFUL AS
A LION IS, SUBJECT ITSELF TO THE INTIMIDATION OF A MAN A WHIP AND A CHAIR? THE
LION HAS BEEN TAUGHT TO FORGET WHAT IT IS. - IYANLA VANZANT

SLEEP	CYCLE	WATER
THRONE	OBSTACLES	INDULGENCES
EXERCISE	STRESS LEVEL	MEDICATION

ELEMENT				SEASON
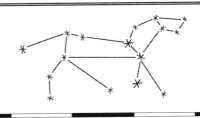 ♌		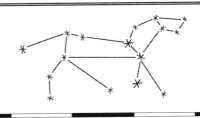	LEO	

August 9, 2019

INTENTION		GRATITUDE
	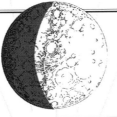	

MEDITATION	WEATHER	MOOD

REMEMBER THAT SOMETIMES NOT GETTING WHAT YOU WANT IS A
WONDERFUL STROKE OF LUCK. - DALAI LAMA

SLEEP	CYCLE	WATER
THRONE	OBSTACLES	INDULGENCES
EXERCISE	STRESS LEVEL	MEDICATION

ELEMENT		SEASON
	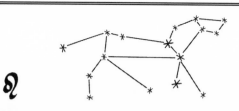 ♌ LEO	

August 10, 2019

INTENTION		GRATITUDE
	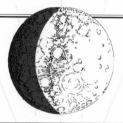	

MEDITATION	WEATHER	MOOD

LOVE IS WHAT WE ARE BORN WITH. FEAR IS WHAT WE LEARN. THE
SPIRITUAL JOURNEY IS THE UNLEARNING OF FEAR AND PREJUDICES AND THE
ACCEPTANCE OF LOVE BACK IN OUR HEARTS. - MARIANNE WILLIAMSON

SLEEP	CYCLE	WATER
THRONE	OBSTACLES	INDULGENCES
EXERCISE	STRESS LEVEL	MEDICATION

ELEMENT				SEASON
♌			LEO	

August 11, 2019

INTENTION		GRATITUDE

MEDITATION	WEATHER	MOOD

SEIZE THE MOMENT AND STAY IN IT.
- LIN-MANUEL MIRANDA

SLEEP	CYCLE	WATER
THRONE	OBSTACLES	INDULGENCES
EXERCISE	STRESS LEVEL	MEDICATION

ELEMENT		LEO	SEASON

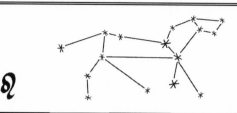

♌

August 12 2019

INTENTION		GRATITUDE

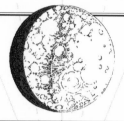

MEDITATION	WEATHER	MOOD

I'VE LEARNED THAT WHENEVER I DECIDE SOMETHING WITH AN OPEN HEART, I
USUALLY MAKE THE RIGHT DECISION. - MAYA ANGELOU

SLEEP	CYCLE	WATER
THRONE	OBSTACLES	INDULGENCES
EXERCISE	STRESS LEVEL	MEDICATION

ELEMENT			SEASON

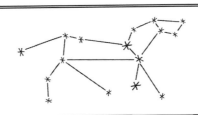

LEO

August 13, 2019

INTENTION		GRATITUDE

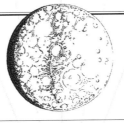

MEDITATION	WEATHER	MOOD

IF YOU ARE IN A BAD MOOD GO FOR A WALK. IF YOU ARE STILL IN A BAD MOOD
GO FOR ANOTHER WALK. - HIPPOCRATES

SLEEP	CYCLE	WATER
THRONE	OBSTACLES	INDULGENCES
EXERCISE	STRESS LEVEL	MEDICATION

ELEMENT			SEASON

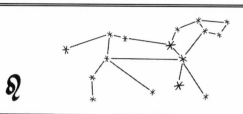

ℒ

LEO

August 14, 2019

INTENTION		GRATITUDE

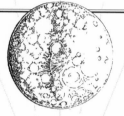

MEDITATION	WEATHER	MOOD

FORGIVENESS IS YOUR RELEASE FROM THE HELL OF WANTING TO KNOW WHAT
CANNOT BE KNOWN AND FROM WANTING TO SEE OTHERS SUFFER BECAUSE
THEY HAVE HURT YOU. - CAROLINE MYSS

SLEEP	CYCLE	WATER
THRONE	OBSTACLES	INDULGENCES
EXERCISE	STRESS LEVEL	MEDICATION

_____
_____
_____
_____
_____
_____
_____
_____
_____
_____
_____

ELEMENT		LEO	SEASON
♌			

August 15, 2019

INTENTION	GRATITUDE

MEDITATION	WEATHER	MOOD

WHEN SOMEONE SHOWS YOU WHO THEY ARE BELIEVE THEM; THE FIRST TIME.
- MAYA ANGELOU

SLEEP	CYCLE	WATER
THRONE	OBSTACLES	INDULGENCES
EXERCISE	STRESS LEVEL	MEDICATION

ELEMENT			SEASON
	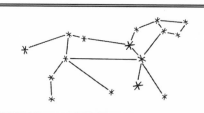	LEO	

August 16, 2019

INTENTION		GRATITUDE
	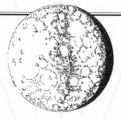	

MEDITATION	WEATHER	MOOD

THE VIBRATION OF YOUR CONSCIOUS INTENT SUPERSEDES ANYTHING THAT
EXISTS IN GROSS PHYSICAL FORM. - FREDDY SILVA

SLEEP	CYCLE	WATER

THRONE	OBSTACLES	INDULGENCES

EXERCISE	STRESS LEVEL	MEDICATION

ELEMENT			SEASON
	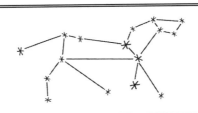 LEO		

August 17, 2019

INTENTION	GRATITUDE

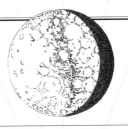

MEDITATION	WEATHER	MOOD

GREAT PEOPLE DO THINGS BEFORE THEY'RE READY. THEY DO THINGS BEFORE
THEY KNOW THEY CAN DO IT. DOING WHAT YOU'RE AFRAID OF, GETTING OUT
OF YOUR COMFORT ZONE, TAKING RISKS LIKE THAT- THAT'S WHAT LIFE IS.
- AMY POEHLER

SLEEP	CYCLE	WATER
THRONE	OBSTACLES	INDULGENCES
EXERCISE	STRESS LEVEL	MEDICATION

ELEMENT			SEASON

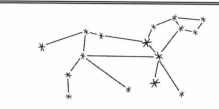

♌

LEO

August 18, 2019

INTENTION		GRATITUDE

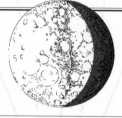

MEDITATION	WEATHER	MOOD

THE MORE YOU PRAISE AND CELEBRATE YOUR LIFE, THE MORE THERE IS IN LIFE
TO CELEBRATE. - OPRAH WINFREY

SLEEP	CYCLE	WATER
THRONE	OBSTACLES	INDULGENCES
EXERCISE	STRESS LEVEL	MEDICATION

_____
_____
_____
_____
_____
_____
_____
_____
_____
_____
_____

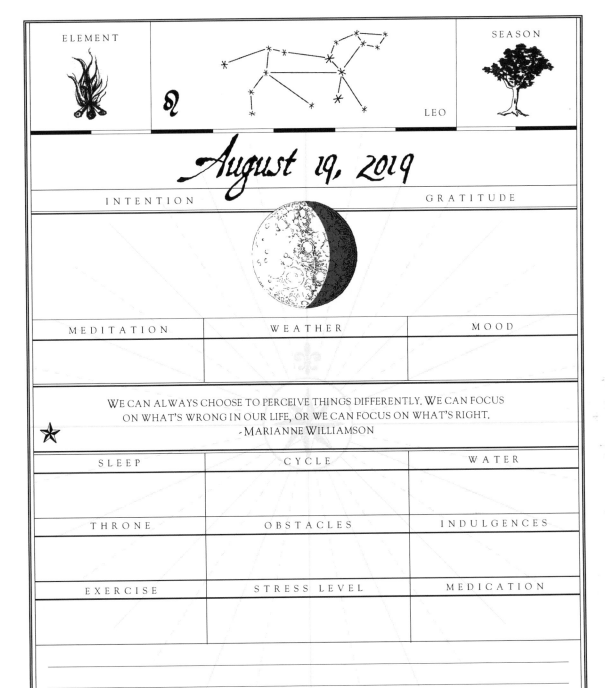

ELEMENT				SEASON

♌

LEO

August 19, 2019

INTENTION	GRATITUDE

MEDITATION	WEATHER	MOOD

WE CAN ALWAYS CHOOSE TO PERCEIVE THINGS DIFFERENTLY. WE CAN FOCUS
ON WHAT'S WRONG IN OUR LIFE, OR WE CAN FOCUS ON WHAT'S RIGHT.
- MARIANNE WILLIAMSON

SLEEP	CYCLE	WATER
THRONE	OBSTACLES	INDULGENCES
EXERCISE	STRESS LEVEL	MEDICATION

ELEMENT	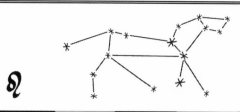	SEASON
♌	LEO	

August 20, 2019

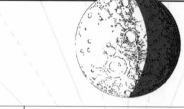

INTENTION		GRATITUDE

MEDITATION	WEATHER	MOOD

OUR BELIEFS CONTROL OUR BODIES, OUR MINDS, AND THUS OUR LIVES.
- DR. BRUCE LIPTON

SLEEP	CYCLE	WATER
THRONE	OBSTACLES	INDULGENCES
EXERCISE	STRESS LEVEL	MEDICATION

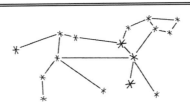
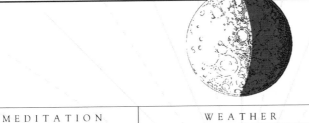

August 21 2019

INTENTION		GRATITUDE

MEDITATION	WEATHER	MOOD

LIVE ONE DAY AT A TIME. KEEP YOUR ATTENTION IN PRESENT TIME. HAVE NO
EXPECTATIONS. MAKE NO JUDGEMENTS. AND GIVE UP THE NEED TO KNOW
WHY THINGS HAPPEN AS THEY DO. GIVE IT UP! - CAROLINE MYSS

SLEEP	CYCLE	WATER
THRONE	OBSTACLES	INDULGENCES
EXERCISE	STRESS LEVEL	MEDICATION

ELEMENT				SEASON

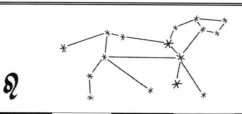

♌

LEO

August 22, 2019

INTENTION		GRATITUDE

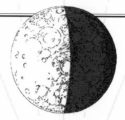

MEDITATION	WEATHER	MOOD

YOUR PERSPECTIVE IS ALWAYS LIMITED BY HOW MUCH YOU KNOW. EXPAND
YOUR KNOWLEDGE AND YOU WILL TRANSFORM YOUR MIND.
- DR. BRUCE LIPTON

SLEEP	CYCLE	WATER
THRONE	OBSTACLES	INDULGENCES
EXERCISE	STRESS LEVEL	MEDICATION

ELEMENT			SEASON

♌

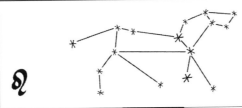

LEO

August 23, 2019

INTENTION		GRATITUDE

MEDITATION	WEATHER	MOOD

IN THE VIBRATION OF APPRECIATION ALL THINGS COME TO YOU. YOU DON'T
HAVE TO MAKE ANYTHING HAPPEN. - ABRAHAM/HICKS

SLEEP	CYCLE	WATER
THRONE	OBSTACLES	INDULGENCES
EXERCISE	STRESS LEVEL	MEDICATION

Virgo

August 29 – September 22

ELEMENT: EARTH

QUALITY: MUTABLE

RULING PLANET: MERCURY

CONSTELLATION: THE VIRGIN

MODE: SENSATION, THOUGHT

MOTTO: "I SERVE"

IN THE GRAND CYCLE OF LIFE: 35-42 YEARS

THEMES:
ORDERLINESS, GROUNDING ENERGY, PERFECTION,
HEALING, STRUCTURE, DISCRIMINATION,
LITERAL INTERPRETATIONS, WIT, THE DETAILS

ELEMENT				SEASON

♍

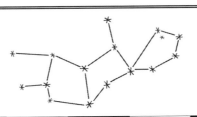

VIRGO

August 29, 2019

INTENTION		GRATITUDE

MEDITATION	WEATHER	MOOD

EVERYTHING WE DO IS INFUSED WITH THE ENERGY WITH WHICH WE DO IT. IF WE'RE
FRANTIC, LIFE WILL BE FRANTIC. IF WE'RE PEACEFUL, LIFE WILL BE PEACEFUL. AND SO OUR
GOAL IN ANY SITUATION BECOMES INNER PEACE. - MARIANNE WILLIAMSON

SLEEP	CYCLE	WATER
THRONE	OBSTACLES	INDULGENCES
EXERCISE	STRESS LEVEL	MEDICATION

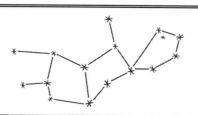

August 25, 2019

INTENTION		GRATITUDE

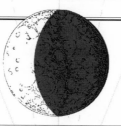

MEDITATION	WEATHER	MOOD

SOONER OR LATER, WE MUST ALL ACCEPT THE FACT THAT IN A RELATIONSHIP,
THE ONLY PERSON YOU ARE DEALING WITH IS YOURSELF. YOUR PARTNER DOES
NOTHING MORE THAN REVEAL YOUR STUFF TO YOU. - IYANLA VANZANT

SLEEP	CYCLE	WATER
THRONE	OBSTACLES	INDULGENCES
EXERCISE	STRESS LEVEL	MEDICATION

ELEMENT			SEASON

 ♍ 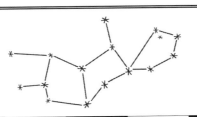 VIRGO

August 26, 2019

INTENTION		GRATITUDE

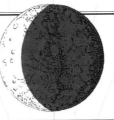

MEDITATION	WEATHER	MOOD

★ IF WE COULD GIVE EVERY INDIVIDUAL THE RIGHT AMOUNT OF NOURISHMENT AND EXERCISE, NOT TOO LITTLE AND NOT TOO MUCH, WE WOULD HAVE FOUND THE SAFEST WAY TO HEALTH. - HIPPOCRATES

SLEEP	CYCLE	WATER
THRONE	OBSTACLES	INDULGENCES
EXERCISE	STRESS LEVEL	MEDICATION

ELEMENT			SEASON

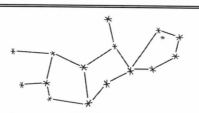

M

VIRGO

August 27, 2019

INTENTION		GRATITUDE

MEDITATION	WEATHER	MOOD

IT'S NEVER OVERREACTING TO ASK FOR WHAT YOU WANT AND NEED.
- AMY POEHLER

SLEEP	CYCLE	WATER
THRONE	OBSTACLES	INDULGENCES
EXERCISE	STRESS LEVEL	MEDICATION

ELEMENT			SEASON
	♍	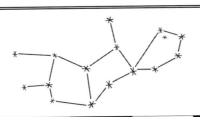 VIRGO	

August 28, 2019

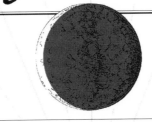

INTENTION		GRATITUDE

MEDITATION	WEATHER	MOOD

WE ARE NOT VICTIMS OF OUR GENES, BUT MASTERS OF OUR FATES, ABLE TO
CREATE LIVES OVERFLOWING WITH PEACE, HAPPINESS, AND LOVE.
- DR. BRUCE LIPTON

SLEEP	CYCLE	WATER
THRONE	OBSTACLES	INDULGENCES
EXERCISE	STRESS LEVEL	MEDICATION

ELEMENT			SEASON

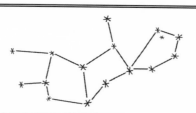

♍

VIRGO

INTENTION		GRATITUDE

MEDITATION	WEATHER	MOOD

NEW MOON HEADS UP! CENTER YOUR INTENTIONS AROUND: IMPROVING YOUR WORK ENVIRONMENT, MAKING POSITIVE CHANGES TO BENEFIT YOUR HEALTH, INCREASING YOUR ABILITY TO SEE THE PLAN THAT WILL BENEFIT YOU, RELEASING THE NEED CRITICIZE.

SLEEP	CYCLE	WATER
THRONE	OBSTACLES	INDULGENCES
EXERCISE	STRESS LEVEL	MEDICATION

The HMS Energy Wheel

New Moon Intentions

ELEMENT			SEASON

 ♍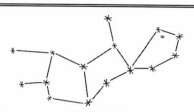

VIRGO

August 30, 2019

INTENTION		GRATITUDE

MEDITATION	WEATHER	MOOD

WE DELIGHT IN THE BEAUTY OF THE BUTTERFLY, BUT RARELY ADMIT THE
CHANGES IT HAS GONE THROUGH TO ACHIEVE THAT BEAUTY.
-MAYA ANGELOU

SLEEP	CYCLE	WATER
THRONE	OBSTACLES	INDULGENCES
EXERCISE	STRESS LEVEL	MEDICATION

ELEMENT			SEASON
	♍	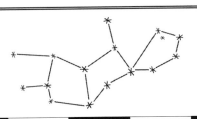 VIRGO	

August 31, 2019

INTENTION		GRATITUDE

MEDITATION	WEATHER	MOOD

FORGIVENESS IS ESSENTIAL TO HEALING, BECAUSE IT REQUIRES YOU TO
SURRENDER YOUR EGO'S NEED TO HAVE LIFE FALL INTO PLACE AROUND YOUR
PERSONAL VERSION OF JUSTICE. - CAROLINE MYSS

SLEEP	CYCLE	WATER
THRONE	OBSTACLES	INDULGENCES
EXERCISE	STRESS LEVEL	MEDICATION

ELEMENT			SEASON

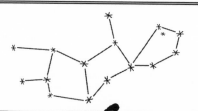

M

VIRGO

September 1, 2019

INTENTION		GRATITUDE

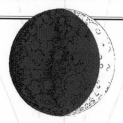

MEDITATION	WEATHER	MOOD

CHOOSE TO BE OPTIMISTIC, IT FEELS BETTER.
- DALAI LAMA

SLEEP	CYCLE	WATER
THRONE	OBSTACLES	INDULGENCES
EXERCISE	STRESS LEVEL	MEDICATION

ELEMENT			SEASON

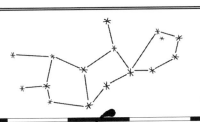

♍

VIRGO

September 2, 2019

INTENTION		GRATITUDE

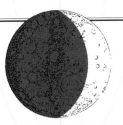

MEDITATION	WEATHER	MOOD

I KEEP LOOKING FOR ONE MORE TEACHER, ONLY TO FIND THAT FISH LEARN
FROM THE WATER AND BIRDS LEARN FROM THE SKY. - MARK NEPO

SLEEP	CYCLE	WATER
THRONE	OBSTACLES	INDULGENCES
EXERCISE	STRESS LEVEL	MEDICATION

ELEMENT		VIRGO	SEASON
 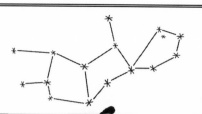 ♍			

September 3, 2019

INTENTION	GRATITUDE

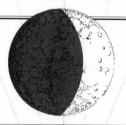

MEDITATION	WEATHER	MOOD

BE THE CHANGE YOU WANT TO SEE IN THE WORLD.
- GANDHI

SLEEP	CYCLE	WATER

THRONE	OBSTACLES	INDULGENCES

EXERCISE	STRESS LEVEL	MEDICATION

September 4, 2019

INTENTION	GRATITUDE

MEDITATION	WEATHER	MOOD

PEOPLE ARE THEIR MOST BEAUTIFUL WHEN THEY ARE LAUGHING, CRYING, DANCING, PLAYING, TELLING THE TRUTH, AND BEING CHASED IN A FUN WAY. - AMY POEHLER

SLEEP	CYCLE	WATER

THRONE	OBSTACLES	INDULGENCES

EXERCISE	STRESS LEVEL	MEDICATION

ELEMENT		VIRGO		SEASON

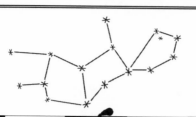

September 5, 2019

INTENTION	GRATITUDE

MEDITATION	WEATHER	MOOD

 I WAS EXHILARATED BY THE NEW REALIZATION THAT I COULD CHANGE THE CHARACTER OF MY LIFE BY CHANGING MY BELIEFS. I WAS INSTANTLY ENERGIZED BECAUSE I REALIZED THAT THERE WAS A SCIENCE-BASED PATH THAT WOULD TAKE ME FROM MY JOB AS A PERENNIAL "VICTIM" TO MY NEW POSITION AS "CO-CREATOR" OF MY DESTINY. - DR. BRUCE LIPTON

SLEEP	CYCLE	WATER
THRONE	OBSTACLES	INDULGENCES
EXERCISE	STRESS LEVEL	MEDICATION

ELEMENT			SEASON

 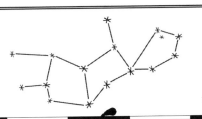

VIRGO

September 6, 2019

INTENTION		GRATITUDE

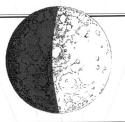

MEDITATION	WEATHER	MOOD

IF YOU ONLY KNEW THE MAGNIFICENCE OF THE 3, 6 AND 9, THEN YOU WOULD
HAVE THE KEY TO THE UNIVERSE. - NIKOLA TESLA

SLEEP	CYCLE	WATER
THRONE	OBSTACLES	INDULGENCES
EXERCISE	STRESS LEVEL	MEDICATION

ELEMENT			SEASON

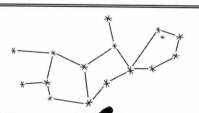

♍

VIRGO

September 7, 2019

INTENTION		GRATITUDE

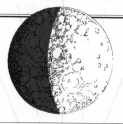

MEDITATION	WEATHER	MOOD

I CAN BE CHANGED BY WHAT HAPPENS TO ME. BUT I REFUSE TO BE REDUCED BY IT.
-MAYA ANGELOU

SLEEP	CYCLE	WATER
THRONE	OBSTACLES	INDULGENCES
EXERCISE	STRESS LEVEL	MEDICATION

ELEMENT			SEASON
	♍	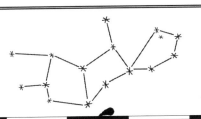 VIRGO	

September 8, 2019

INTENTION		GRATITUDE
	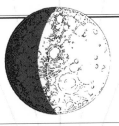	

MEDITATION	WEATHER	MOOD

THE APPRECIATION THAT SOURCE FEELS FOR YOU, NEVER-ENDINGLY, WILL
WRAP YOU IN A WARM BLANKET OF WORTHINESS IF YOU WILL ALLOW IT.
- ABRAHAM/HICKS

SLEEP	CYCLE	WATER
THRONE	OBSTACLES	INDULGENCES
EXERCISE	STRESS LEVEL	MEDICATION

ELEMENT			SEASON

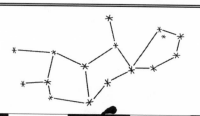

♍

VIRGO

September 9, 2019

INTENTION		GRATITUDE

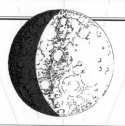

MEDITATION	WEATHER	MOOD

THINK LIKE A QUEEN. A QUEEN IS NOT AFRAID TO FAIL. FAILURE IS ANOTHER
STEPPING STONE TO GREATNESS. - OPRAH WINFREY

SLEEP	CYCLE	WATER
THRONE	OBSTACLES	INDULGENCES
EXERCISE	STRESS LEVEL	MEDICATION

ELEMENT			SEASON

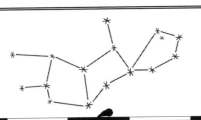

♍

VIRGO

September 10, 2019

INTENTION		GRATITUDE

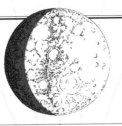

MEDITATION	WEATHER	MOOD

THE SEPARATION BETWEEN US AND THEM OR BETWEEN US AND NATURE THAT WE SO
VIVIDLY EXPERIENCE IN OUR REALITY IS AN ILLUSION HELD IN PLACE BY OUR BELIEFS.
- DR. BRUCE LIPTON

SLEEP	CYCLE	WATER
THRONE	OBSTACLES	INDULGENCES
EXERCISE	STRESS LEVEL	MEDICATION

ELEMENT				SEASON
	♍	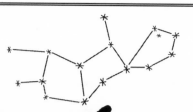	VIRGO	

September 11, 2019

INTENTION		GRATITUDE

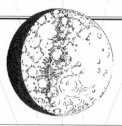

MEDITATION	WEATHER	MOOD

THE PRACTICE OF FORGIVENESS IS OUR MOST IMPORTANT CONTRIBUTION TO
THE HEALING OF THE WORLD. - MARIANNE WILLIAMSON

SLEEP	CYCLE	WATER
THRONE	OBSTACLES	INDULGENCES
EXERCISE	STRESS LEVEL	MEDICATION

_____
_____
_____
_____
_____
_____
_____
_____
_____
_____

ELEMENT		SEASON
 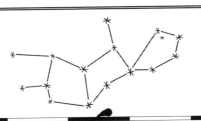	VIRGO	

September 12, 2019

INTENTION		GRATITUDE
	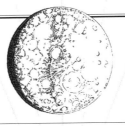	

MEDITATION	WEATHER	MOOD

YOU HAVE TO CARE ABOUT YOUR WORK BUT NOT ABOUT THE RESULT. YOU HAVE TO CARE ABOUT HOW GOOD YOU ARE AND HOW GOOD YOU FEEL, BUT NOT ABOUT HOW GOOD PEOPLE THINK YOU ARE OR HOW GOOD PEOPLE THINK YOU LOOK. - AMY POEHLER

SLEEP	CYCLE	WATER
THRONE	OBSTACLES	INDULGENCES
EXERCISE	STRESS LEVEL	MEDICATION

ELEMENT		SEASON
	♍ VIRGO	

September 13, 2019

INTENTION		GRATITUDE

MEDITATION	WEATHER	MOOD

UNTIL AND UNLESS YOU KNOW THAT YOU ARE ENOUGH JUST THE WAY YOU ARE, YOU WILL ALWAYS BE DRIVEN TO LOOK FOR MORE. KNOWING THAT YOU ARE ENOUGH IS A FUNCTION OF CONSCIOUSNESS. YOUR ENOUGH-NESS DEVELOPS IN DIRECT PROPORTION TO THE RELATIONSHIP YOU HAVE WITH YOUR TRUE IDENTITY. - IYANLA VANZANT

SLEEP	CYCLE	WATER
THRONE	OBSTACLES	INDULGENCES
EXERCISE	STRESS LEVEL	MEDICATION

ELEMENT			SEASON
	♍	 VIRGO	

September 14, 2019

INTENTION		GRATITUDE

MEDITATION	WEATHER	MOOD

THE HARD THINGS BREAK. THE SOFT THINGS BEND. THE STUBBORN ONES
BATTER THEMSELVES AGAINST ALL THAT IS IMMOVABLE. THE FLEXIBLE ADAPT
TO WHAT IS BEFORE THEM. - MARK NEPO

SLEEP	CYCLE	WATER
THRONE	OBSTACLES	INDULGENCES
EXERCISE	STRESS LEVEL	MEDICATION

ELEMENT				SEASON

♍

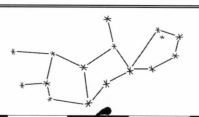

VIRGO

September 15, 2019

INTENTION	GRATITUDE

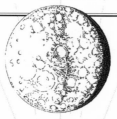

MEDITATION	WEATHER	MOOD

HEALING COMES FROM GATHERING WISDOM FROM PAST ACTIONS AND
LETTING GO OF THE PAIN THAT THE EDUCATION COST YOU.
- CAROLINE MYSS

SLEEP	CYCLE	WATER
THRONE	OBSTACLES	INDULGENCES
EXERCISE	STRESS LEVEL	MEDICATION

ELEMENT		VIRGO	SEASON

September 16, 2019

INTENTION		GRATITUDE

MEDITATION	WEATHER	MOOD

CELLS, TISSUES, AND ORGANS DO NOT QUESTION INFORMATION SENT BY THE NERVOUS SYSTEM. RATHER, THEY RESPOND WITH EQUAL FERVOR TO ACCURATE LIFE-AFFIRMING PERCEPTIONS AND TO SELF-DESTRUCTIVE MISPERCEPTIONS. CONSEQUENTLY, THE NATURE OF OUR PERCEPTIONS GREATLY INFLUENCES THE FATE OF OUR LIVES. - DR. BRUCE LIPTON

SLEEP	CYCLE	WATER
THRONE	OBSTACLES	INDULGENCES
EXERCISE	STRESS LEVEL	MEDICATION

ELEMENT		VIRGO		SEASON

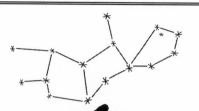

♍

VIRGO

September 17, 2019

INTENTION	GRATITUDE

MEDITATION	WEATHER	MOOD

I AM INTRODUCING A NEW IDEA. TRY TO CARE LESS. PRACTICE AMBIVALENCE.
LEARN TO LET GO OF WANTING IT. - AMY POEHLER

SLEEP	CYCLE	WATER
THRONE	OBSTACLES	INDULGENCES
EXERCISE	STRESS LEVEL	MEDICATION

ELEMENT			SEASON

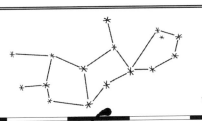

♍

VIRGO

September 18, 2019

INTENTION		GRATITUDE

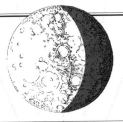

MEDITATION	WEATHER	MOOD

★ FEW REALIZE THAT THEY CAN CONTROL THE WAY THEY FEEL AND POSITIVELY
AFFECT THE THINGS THAT COME INTO THEIR LIFE EXPERIENCE BY DELIBERATELY
DIRECTING THEIR THOUGHTS. - ABRAHAM/HICKS

SLEEP	CYCLE	WATER
THRONE	OBSTACLES	INDULGENCES
EXERCISE	STRESS LEVEL	MEDICATION

ELEMENT				SEASON

♍

VIRGO

September 19, 2019

INTENTION		GRATITUDE

MEDITATION	WEATHER	MOOD

THOSE WHO TRULY LOVE US WILL NEVER KNOWINGLY ASK US TO BE OTHER THAN WE ARE.
-MARK NEPO

SLEEP	CYCLE	WATER
THRONE	OBSTACLES	INDULGENCES
EXERCISE	STRESS LEVEL	MEDICATION

ELEMENT				SEASON

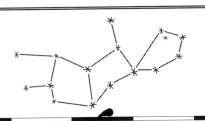

♍

VIRGO

September 20, 2019

INTENTION		GRATITUDE

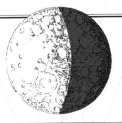

MEDITATION	WEATHER	MOOD

BY LEARNING TO IDENTIFY YOUR ENERGY PATTERNS, YOU WILL BE ABLE TO
GAIN A MUCH GREATER VISION OF THE MEANING AND PURPOSE OF YOUR
MANY EXPERIENCES AND RELATIONSHIPS. - CAROLINE MYSS

SLEEP	CYCLE	WATER
THRONE	OBSTACLES	INDULGENCES
EXERCISE	STRESS LEVEL	MEDICATION

ELEMENT			SEASON

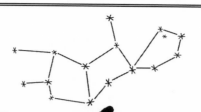

♍

VIRGO

September 21, 2019

INTENTION	GRATITUDE

MEDITATION	WEATHER	MOOD

NO ONE IS FIXED UNTIL THEY MAKE THE EFFORT TO CHANGE.
- DR. BRUCE LIPTON

SLEEP	CYCLE	WATER
THRONE	OBSTACLES	INDULGENCES
EXERCISE	STRESS LEVEL	MEDICATION

ELEMENT			SEASON

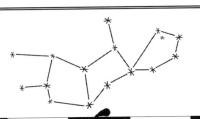

♍

VIRGO

September 22, 2019

INTENTION		GRATITUDE

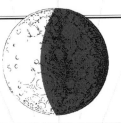

MEDITATION	WEATHER	MOOD

THE DESIRE TO REACH FOR THE STARS IS AMBITIOUS. THE DESIRE TO REACH
HEARTS IS WISE. - MAYA ANGELOU

SLEEP	CYCLE	WATER
THRONE	OBSTACLES	INDULGENCES
EXERCISE	STRESS LEVEL	MEDICATION

Libra

September 23 – October 22

ELEMENT: AIR

QUALITY: CARDINAL

RULING PLANET: VENUS

CONSTELLATION: THE SCALES

MODE: THOUGHT, SENSATION

MOTTO: "I WEIGH"

IN THE GRAND CYCLE OF LIFE: 42-49 YEARS

THEMES:
JUSTICE, INDECISION, CHARM, GRACE,
HUMOR, BEAUTY, SOCIAL ACTIVITY, ROMANCE,
NEGOTIATION, EQUALITY

ELEMENT		LIBRA	SEASON

September 23, 2019

INTENTION		GRATITUDE

Autumnal *Equinox*

MEDITATION	WEATHER	MOOD

WE ARE NOT HELD BACK BY THE LOVE WE DIDN'T RECEIVE IN THE PAST, BUT BY
THE LOVE WE'RE NOT EXTENDING IN THE PRESENT. - MARIANNE WILLIAMSON

SLEEP	CYCLE	WATER
THRONE	OBSTACLES	INDULGENCES
EXERCISE	STRESS LEVEL	MEDICATION

_____
_____
_____
_____
_____
_____
_____
_____
_____
_____
_____
_____

ELEMENT			SEASON

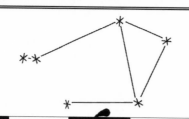

LIBRA

September 29, 2019

INTENTION		GRATITUDE

MEDITATION	WEATHER	MOOD

I AM CONVINCED THAT THE DEEPEST DESIRE WITHIN EACH OF US IS TO BE
LIBERATED FROM THE CONTROLLING INFLUENCES OF OUR OWN PSYCHIC
MADNESS OR PATTERNS OF FEAR. - CAROLINE MYSS

SLEEP	CYCLE	WATER
THRONE	OBSTACLES	INDULGENCES
EXERCISE	STRESS LEVEL	MEDICATION

September 25, 2019

INTENTION		GRATITUDE

MEDITATION	WEATHER	MOOD

DECIDE WHAT YOUR CURRENCY IS EARLY, LET GO OF WHAT YOU WILL NEVER HAVE. PEOPLE WHO DO THIS ARE HAPPIER AND SEXIER. - AMY POEHLER

SLEEP	CYCLE	WATER
THRONE	OBSTACLES	INDULGENCES
EXERCISE	STRESS LEVEL	MEDICATION

ELEMENT				SEASON

 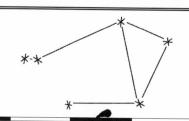

LIBRA

September 26, 2019

INTENTION	GRATITUDE

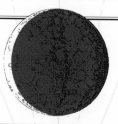

MEDITATION	WEATHER	MOOD

IF YOU RETAIN NOTHING ELSE, ALWAYS REMEMBER THE MOST IMPORTANT
RULE OF BEAUTY, WHICH IS: WHO CARES? - TINA FEY

SLEEP	CYCLE	WATER
THRONE	OBSTACLES	INDULGENCES
EXERCISE	STRESS LEVEL	MEDICATION

ELEMENT		SEASON

♎ LIBRA

September 27, 2019

INTENTION		GRATITUDE

MEDITATION	WEATHER	MOOD

New Moon Heads Up! Center your intentions around: Improving Existing Relationships, Improving Social Skills, Attracting a Suitable Life Partner, Enhancing Self-confidence.

SLEEP	CYCLE	WATER
THRONE	OBSTACLES	INDULGENCES
EXERCISE	STRESS LEVEL	MEDICATION

The HMS Energy Wheel

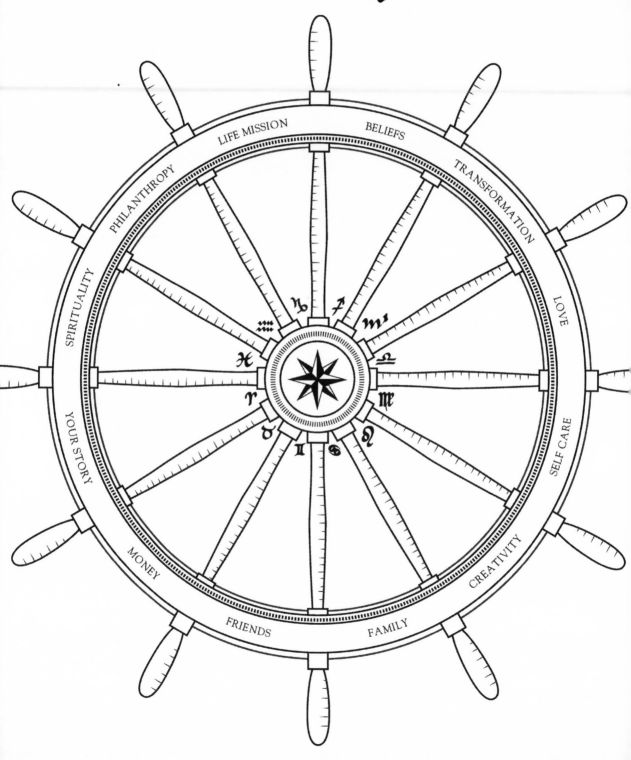

New Moon Intentions

2:26PM EST

New Moon Intentions

ELEMENT		SEASON

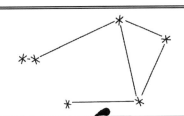

LIBRA

September 28, 2019

INTENTION	GRATITUDE

MEDITATION	WEATHER	MOOD

IT IS NOT YOUR JOB TO MAKE SOMETHING HAPPEN—UNIVERSAL FORCES ARE IN PLACE FOR ALL OF THAT. YOUR WORK IS TO SIMPLY DETERMINE WHAT YOU WANT.
- ABRAHAM/HICKS

SLEEP	CYCLE	WATER
THRONE	OBSTACLES	INDULGENCES
EXERCISE	STRESS LEVEL	MEDICATION

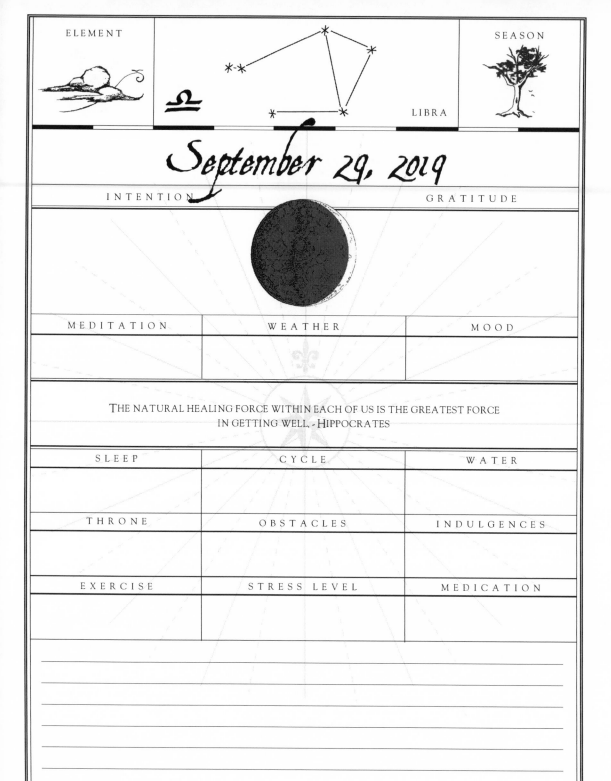

ELEMENT

LIBRA

SEASON

September 29, 2019

| INTENTION | GRATITUDE |

| MEDITATION | WEATHER | MOOD |

THE NATURAL HEALING FORCE WITHIN EACH OF US IS THE GREATEST FORCE
IN GETTING WELL. - HIPPOCRATES

| SLEEP | CYCLE | WATER |

| THRONE | OBSTACLES | INDULGENCES |

| EXERCISE | STRESS LEVEL | MEDICATION |

September 30, 2019

INTENTION

GRATITUDE

MEDITATION

WEATHER

MOOD

> YOU NEED TO CHALLENGE YOUR FEAR OF LIFE BECOMING UNREASONABLE - BECAUSE IT IS ALREADY UNREASONABLE. IN TRUTH, YOUR LIFE HAS NEVER BEEN REASONABLE, IT'S JUST THAT YOU KEEP HOPING TOMORROW WILL BE DIFFERENT AND THAT YOU WILL FIND A WAY TO BRING MORE CONTROL INTO YOUR WORLD. - CAROLINE MYSS

SLEEP

CYCLE

WATER

THRONE

OBSTACLES

INDULGENCES

EXERCISE

STRESS LEVEL

MEDICATION

ELEMENT				SEASON

LIBRA

October 1, 2019

INTENTION		GRATITUDE

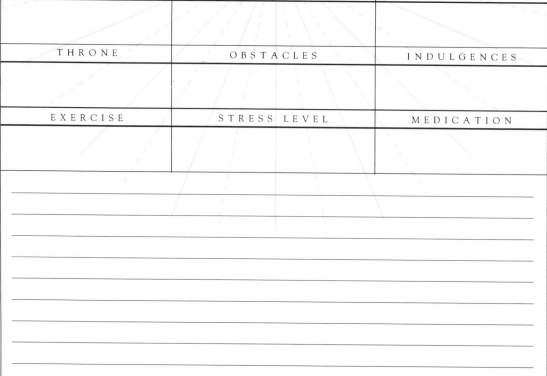

MEDITATION	WEATHER	MOOD

YOU MAY BELIEVE THAT YOU ARE RESPONSIBLE FOR WHAT YOU DO, BUT NOT FOR WHAT YOU THINK. THE TRUTH IS THAT YOU ARE RESPONSIBLE FOR WHAT YOU THINK, BECAUSE IT IS ONLY AT THIS LEVEL THAT YOU CAN EXERCISE CHOICE. WHAT YOU DO COMES FROM WHAT YOU THINK. - MARIANNE WILLIAMSON

SLEEP	CYCLE	WATER
THRONE	OBSTACLES	INDULGENCES
EXERCISE	STRESS LEVEL	MEDICATION

October 2, 2019

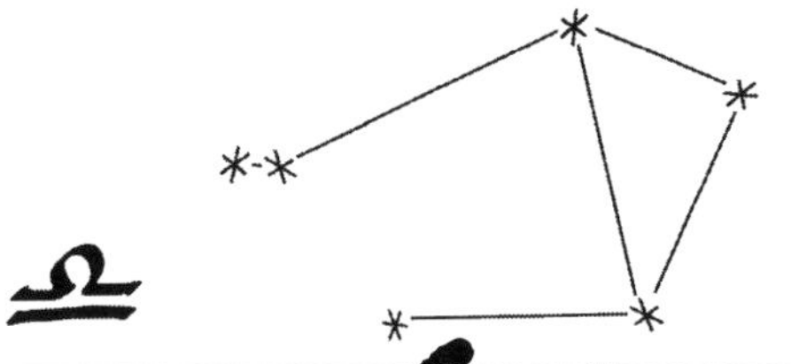

INTENTION

GRATITUDE

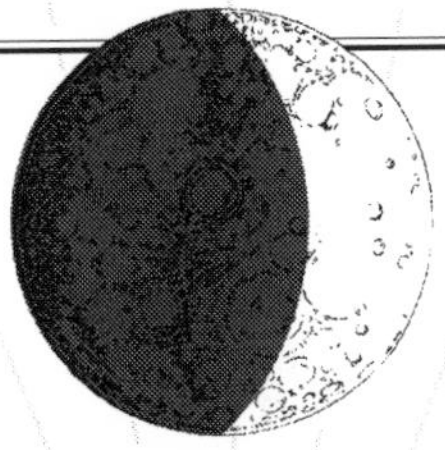

MEDITATION	WEATHER	MOOD

GRACE IS A POWER THAT COMES IN AND TRANSFORMS A MOMENT INTO
SOMETHING BETTER. - CAROLINE MYSS

SLEEP	CYCLE	WATER
THRONE	OBSTACLES	INDULGENCES
EXERCISE	STRESS LEVEL	MEDICATION

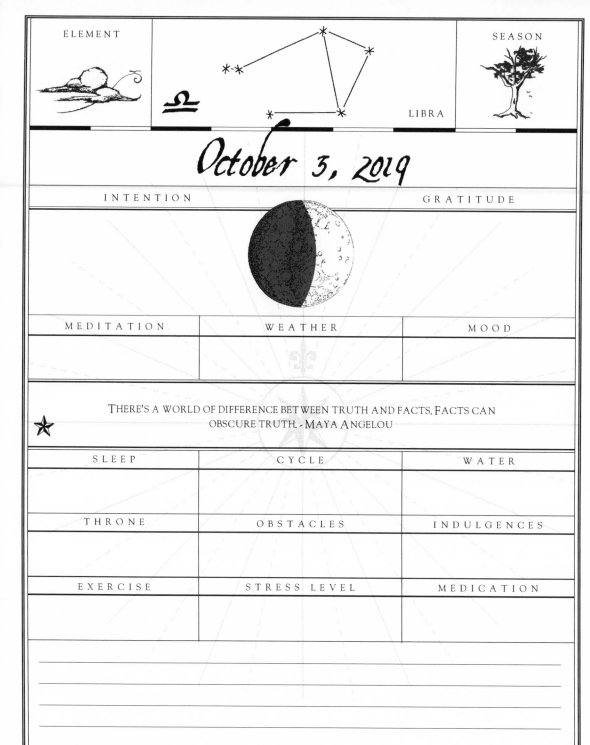

ELEMENT

SEASON

LIBRA

October 3, 2019

INTENTION

GRATITUDE

MEDITATION	WEATHER	MOOD

THERE'S A WORLD OF DIFFERENCE BETWEEN TRUTH AND FACTS. FACTS CAN
OBSCURE TRUTH. - MAYA ANGELOU

SLEEP	CYCLE	WATER
THRONE	OBSTACLES	INDULGENCES
EXERCISE	STRESS LEVEL	MEDICATION

♎︎

LIBRA

October 4, 2019

INTENTION

GRATITUDE

MEDITATION	WEATHER	MOOD

I LEARNED AGAIN AND AGAIN IN MY LIFE, UNTIL YOU GET YOUR OWN ACT
TOGETHER, YOU'RE NOT READY FOR BIG LOVE. WHAT YOU'RE READY FOR IS
ONE OF THOSE CODEPENDENT RELATIONSHIPS WHERE YOU DESPERATELY NEED
A PARTNER. - DR. BRUCE LIPTON

SLEEP	CYCLE	WATER
THRONE	OBSTACLES	INDULGENCES
EXERCISE	STRESS LEVEL	MEDICATION

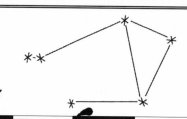

LIBRA

October 5, 2019

INTENTION		GRATITUDE

MEDITATION	WEATHER	MOOD

THE ONLY WAY WE WILL SURVIVE IS BY BEING KIND. THE ONLY WAY WE CAN GET BY IN THIS WORLD IS THROUGH THE HELP WE RECEIVE FROM OTHERS. NO ONE CAN DO IT ALONE, NO MATTER HOW GREAT THE MACHINES ARE. - AMY POEHLER

SLEEP	CYCLE	WATER
THRONE	OBSTACLES	INDULGENCES
EXERCISE	STRESS LEVEL	MEDICATION

October 6, 2019

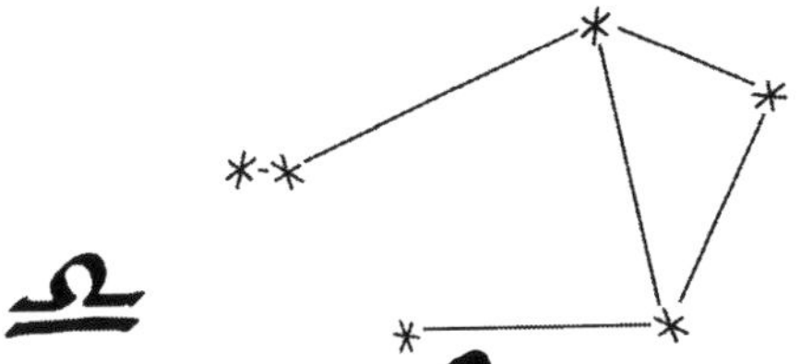

INTENTION

GRATITUDE

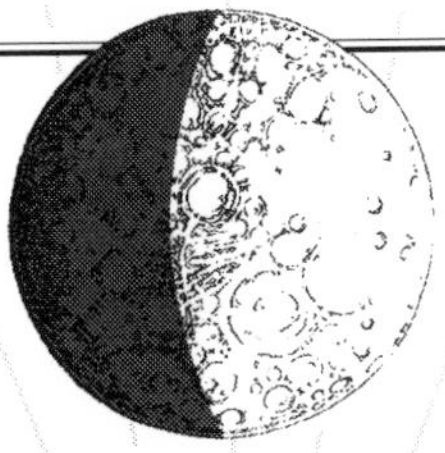

MEDITATION

WEATHER

MOOD

YOUR EMOTIONS ARE THE SLAVES TO YOUR THOUGHTS, AND YOU ARE THE
SLAVE TO YOUR EMOTIONS. - ELIZABETH GILBERT

SLEEP

CYCLE

WATER

THRONE

OBSTACLES

INDULGENCES

EXERCISE

STRESS LEVEL

MEDICATION

ELEMENT			SEASON

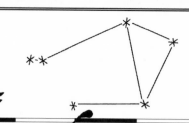

LIBRA

October 7, 2019

INTENTION		GRATITUDE

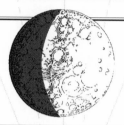

MEDITATION	WEATHER	MOOD

LOVE IS THE ESSENTIAL EXISTENTIAL FACT. IT IS OUR ULTIMATE REALITY AND OUR PURPOSE ON EARTH. TO BE CONSCIOUSLY AWARE OF IT, TO EXPERIENCE LOVE IN OURSELVES AND OTHERS, IS THE MEANING OF LIFE. - MARIANNE WILLIAMSON

SLEEP	CYCLE	WATER
THRONE	OBSTACLES	INDULGENCES
EXERCISE	STRESS LEVEL	MEDICATION

LIBRA

October 8, 2019

INTENTION

GRATITUDE

MEDITATION

WEATHER

MOOD

MANIPULATION IS THE ART OF MAKING ANOTHER PERSON'S SPIRIT DANCE
FOR PERSONAL AMUSEMENT, AND ONLY THROUGH HONORING ONESELF DO WE
BECOME STRONG ENOUGH TO REFUSE TO DANCE. - CAROLINE MYSS

SLEEP

CYCLE

WATER

THRONE

OBSTACLES

INDULGENCES

EXERCISE

STRESS LEVEL

MEDICATION

October 9, 2019

INTENTION		GRATITUDE

MEDITATION	WEATHER	MOOD

IT TAKES YEARS AS A WOMAN TO UNLEARN WHAT YOU HAVE BEEN TAUGHT TO BE SORRY FOR. IT TAKES YEARS TO FIND YOUR VOICE AND SEIZE YOUR REAL ESTATE. - AMY POEHLER

SLEEP	CYCLE	WATER
THRONE	OBSTACLES	INDULGENCES
EXERCISE	STRESS LEVEL	MEDICATION

October 10, 2019

INTENTION		GRATITUDE

MEDITATION	WEATHER	MOOD

I'D RATHER BE A FAILURE AT SOMETHING I LOVE THAN A SUCCESS AT
SOMETHING I HATE. - GEORGE BURNS

SLEEP	CYCLE	WATER
THRONE	OBSTACLES	INDULGENCES
EXERCISE	STRESS LEVEL	MEDICATION

ELEMENT		SEASON
	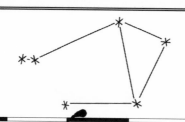 LIBRA	

October 11, 2019

INTENTION		GRATITUDE
	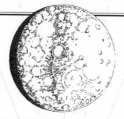	

MEDITATION	WEATHER	MOOD

 CHALLENGES ARE GIFTS THAT FORCE US TO SEARCH FOR A NEW CENTER OF GRAVITY. DON'T FIGHT THEM, JUST FIND A NEW WAY TO STAND.
- OPRAH WINFREY

SLEEP	CYCLE	WATER
THRONE	OBSTACLES	INDULGENCES
EXERCISE	STRESS LEVEL	MEDICATION

_____

_____

_____

_____

_____

_____

_____

_____

October 12, 2019

INTENTION		GRATITUDE

MEDITATION	WEATHER	MOOD

I'VE LEARNED WE ALL GET EXACTLY WHAT WE NEED, WHEN WE NEED IT, IN
ORDER TO LEARN WHAT GOD INTENDS FOR US TO KNOW SO WE CAN BE WHO
GOD INTENDS FOR US TO BE. - IYANLA VANZANT

SLEEP	CYCLE	WATER
THRONE	OBSTACLES	INDULGENCES
EXERCISE	STRESS LEVEL	MEDICATION

ELEMENT		SEASON

LIBRA

October 13, 2019

INTENTION	GRATITUDE

MEDITATION	WEATHER	MOOD

MY GREAT HOPE IS TO LAUGH AS MUCH AS I CRY; TO GET MY WORK DONE AND TRY TO LOVE
SOMEBODY AND HAVE THE COURAGE TO ACCEPT THE LOVE IN RETURN. - MAYA ANGELOU

SLEEP	CYCLE	WATER
THRONE	OBSTACLES	INDULGENCES
EXERCISE	STRESS LEVEL	MEDICATION

_____
_____
_____
_____
_____
_____
_____
_____
_____
_____

October 14, 2019

INTENTION		GRATITUDE

MEDITATION	WEATHER	MOOD

BUT TODAY YOU ARE PRECIOUS AND RARE AND AWAKE. IT USHERS US INTO
GRATEFUL LIVING. IT MAKES HESITATION USELESS. GRATEFUL AND AWAKE,
ASK WHAT YOU NEED TO KNOW NOW. SAY WHAT YOU FEEL NOW. LOVE WHAT
YOU LOVE NOW. - MARK NEPO

SLEEP	CYCLE	WATER
THRONE	OBSTACLES	INDULGENCES
EXERCISE	STRESS LEVEL	MEDICATION

October 15, 2019

INTENTION		GRATITUDE

MEDITATION	WEATHER	MOOD

SOMETHING AMAZING HAPPENS WHEN WE SURRENDER AND JUST LOVE. WE MELT
INTO ANOTHER WORLD, A REALM OF POWER ALREADY WITHIN US. THE WORLD
CHANGES WHEN WE CHANGE. THE WORLD SOFTENS WHEN WE SOFTEN. THE WORLD
LOVES US WHEN WE CHOOSE TO LOVE THE WORLD. - MARIANNE WILLIAMSON

SLEEP	CYCLE	WATER

THRONE	OBSTACLES	INDULGENCES

EXERCISE	STRESS LEVEL	MEDICATION

October 16, 2019

INTENTION		GRATITUDE

MEDITATION	WEATHER	MOOD

YOU CAN GET TO WHERE YOU WANT TO BE FROM WHEREVER YOU ARE—BUT
YOU MUST STOP SPENDING SO MUCH TIME NOTICING AND TALKING ABOUT
WHAT YOU DO NOT LIKE ABOUT WHERE YOU ARE. - ABRAHAM/HICKS

SLEEP	CYCLE	WATER
THRONE	OBSTACLES	INDULGENCES
EXERCISE	STRESS LEVEL	MEDICATION

ELEMENT		LIBRA		SEASON

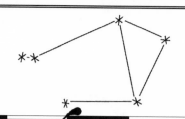

October 17, 2019

INTENTION		GRATITUDE

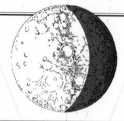

MEDITATION	WEATHER	MOOD

SELL YOUR CLEVERNESS AND BUY BEWILDERMENT.
- RUMI

SLEEP	CYCLE	WATER
THRONE	OBSTACLES	INDULGENCES
EXERCISE	STRESS LEVEL	MEDICATION

October 18, 2019

INTENTION		GRATITUDE

MEDITATION	WEATHER	MOOD

THE JOURNEY OF LIFE IS THE UNIFICATION OF FRAGMENTATION. FRAGMENTS
ARE UNITS OF POWER THAT ARE OUT OF CONTROL. WE MAKE AGREEMENTS TO
COME AND COLLECT OURSELVES. - CAROLINE MYSS

SLEEP	CYCLE	WATER
THRONE	OBSTACLES	INDULGENCES
EXERCISE	STRESS LEVEL	MEDICATION

ELEMENT			SEASON

 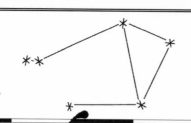

LIBRA

October 19, 2019

INTENTION		GRATITUDE

MEDITATION	WEATHER	MOOD

TRUE FREEDOM MEANS THAT YOU ARE NOT OBSTRUCTED BY THE CONDITIONS
CONSTRAINTS AND CONCERNS THAT OTHERS TRY AND IMPOSE ON YOU.
- DAVID WILCOCK

SLEEP	CYCLE	WATER
THRONE	OBSTACLES	INDULGENCES
EXERCISE	STRESS LEVEL	MEDICATION

ELEMENT			SEASON

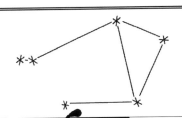

LIBRA

October 20, 2019

INTENTION	GRATITUDE

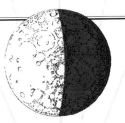

MEDITATION	WEATHER	MOOD

SPIRITUAL GROWTH INVOLVES GIVING UP THE STORIES OF YOUR PAST SO THE
UNIVERSE CAN WRITE A NEW ONE. - MARIANNE WILLIAMSON

SLEEP	CYCLE	WATER
THRONE	OBSTACLES	INDULGENCES
EXERCISE	STRESS LEVEL	MEDICATION

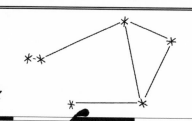

October 21, 2019

INTENTION		GRATITUDE

MEDITATION	WEATHER	MOOD

HUMAN BEINGS ARE NOT MEANT TO LIVE ALONE. THERE IS A FUNDAMENTAL
BIOLOGICAL IMPERATIVE THAT PROPELS YOU AND EVERY ORGANISM ON
THIS PLANET TO BE IN A COMMUNITY, TO BE IN RELATIONSHIP WITH OTHER
ORGANISMS. - DR. BRUCE LIPTON

SLEEP	CYCLE	WATER
THRONE	OBSTACLES	INDULGENCES
EXERCISE	STRESS LEVEL	MEDICATION

October 22, 2019

INTENTION		GRATITUDE

MEDITATION	WEATHER	MOOD

I DID THEN WHAT I KNEW HOW TO DO. NOW THAT I KNOW BETTER, I DO BETTER.
- MAYA ANGELOU

SLEEP	CYCLE	WATER
THRONE	OBSTACLES	INDULGENCES
EXERCISE	STRESS LEVEL	MEDICATION

Scorpio

October 23 – November 21

ELEMENT: WATER

QUALITY: FIXED

RULING PLANET: PLUTO

CONSTELLATION: THE SCORPION

MODE: FEELING

MOTTO: "I CONTROL"

IN THE GRAND CYCLE OF LIFE: 49-56 YEARS

THEMES:
METAMORPHOSIS, TRANSFORMATION,
DOMINATION, ATTACHMENT, POWER,
DEFENSIVENESS, INTERNALIZATION, THE SHADOW

October 23, 2019

INTENTION

GRATITUDE

MEDITATION

WEATHER

MOOD

YOU KNOW WHY IT'S HARD TO BE HAPPY — IT'S BECAUSE WE REFUSE TO LET GO
OF THE THINGS THAT MAKE US SAD. - DR. BRUCE LIPTON

SLEEP

CYCLE

WATER

THRONE

OBSTACLES

INDULGENCES

EXERCISE

STRESS LEVEL

MEDICATION

ELEMENT			SEASON

m'

SCORPIO

October 24, 2019

INTENTION		GRATITUDE

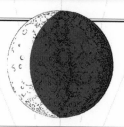

MEDITATION	WEATHER	MOOD

WHEN A WOMAN RISES UP IN GLORY, HER ENERGY IS MAGNETIC AND HER
SENSE OF POSSIBILITY CONTAGIOUS. - MARIANNE WILLIAMSON

SLEEP	CYCLE	WATER
THRONE	OBSTACLES	INDULGENCES
EXERCISE	STRESS LEVEL	MEDICATION

October 25, 2019

INTENTION		GRATITUDE

MEDITATION	WEATHER	MOOD

DO NOT APOLOGIZE FOR CRYING. WITHOUT THIS EMOTION, WE ARE ONLY ROBOTS.
- ELIZABETH GILBERT

SLEEP	CYCLE	WATER
THRONE	OBSTACLES	INDULGENCES
EXERCISE	STRESS LEVEL	MEDICATION

ELEMENT		SCORPIO	SEASON
	♏ ⁂		

October 26, 2019

INTENTION		GRATITUDE

MEDITATION	WEATHER	MOOD

NEW MOON HEADS UP! CENTER YOUR INTENTIONS AROUND: PERSONAL & BUSINESS RELATIONSHIPS, DEBT RESOLUTION, INCREASING PSYCHIC & PSYCHOLOGICAL ABILITIES

SLEEP	CYCLE	WATER

THRONE	OBSTACLES	INDULGENCES

EXERCISE	STRESS LEVEL	MEDICATION

The HMS Energy Wheel

New Moon Intentions

ELEMENT		SCORPIO	SEASON

October 27, 2019

INTENTION	GRATITUDE

MEDITATION	WEATHER	MOOD

⭐ AS THE BUDDHA TAUGHT, THE CAUSE OF SUFFERING IS ATTACHMENT; THE
END OF ATTACHMENT WILL MEAN THE END OF SUFFERING. - CAROLINE MYSS

SLEEP	CYCLE	WATER
THRONE	OBSTACLES	INDULGENCES
EXERCISE	STRESS LEVEL	MEDICATION

ELEMENT		SEASON
	 SCORPIO	

INTENTION		GRATITUDE

MEDITATION	WEATHER	MOOD

HAPPINESS IS THE CHOICE I MAKE TODAY. IT DOES NOT REST ON MY CIRCUMSTANCES, BUT ON MY FRAME OF MIND. I SURRENDER TO GOD ANY EMOTIONAL HABITS THAT LEAD ME DOWN THE PATH OF UNHAPPINESS, AND PRAY FOR GUIDANCE IN SHIFTING MY THOUGHTS. - MARIANNE WILLIAMSON

SLEEP	CYCLE	WATER
THRONE	OBSTACLES	INDULGENCES
EXERCISE	STRESS LEVEL	MEDICATION

ELEMENT		SEASON

m SCORPIO

October 29, 2019

INTENTION	GRATITUDE

MEDITATION	WEATHER	MOOD

BREATHE LIKE A FALLEN LEAF AND THINK OF NOTHING. JUST BREATHE AND
LET YOUR HEART AND MIND BE CARRIED, HOWEVER BRIEFLY, BY THE SPIRIT
YOU CAN'T QUITE SEE. - MARK NEPO

SLEEP	CYCLE	WATER
THRONE	OBSTACLES	INDULGENCES
EXERCISE	STRESS LEVEL	MEDICATION

♏

SCORPIO

October 30, 2019

INTENTION		GRATITUDE

MEDITATION	WEATHER	MOOD

EVEN THOUGH THERE IS A PART OF ME HOLDING ON TO THE BELIEF THAT I AM NOW, HAVE ALWAYS BEEN, AND WILL ALWAYS BE UNWORTHY, I AM STILL WILLING TO LOVE AND ACCEPT MYSELF. - IYANLA VANZANT

SLEEP	CYCLE	WATER
THRONE	OBSTACLES	INDULGENCES
EXERCISE	STRESS LEVEL	MEDICATION

ELEMENT				SEASON

M

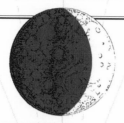

SCORPIO

October 31, 2019

INTENTION	GRATITUDE

MEDITATION	WEATHER	MOOD

SUPERSTITION IS WHAT REMAINS AFTER THE ORIGINAL UNDERSTANDING OF
A CONCEPT HAS BEEN LOST OVER TIME. - FREDDY SILVA

SLEEP	CYCLE	WATER
THRONE	OBSTACLES	INDULGENCES
EXERCISE	STRESS LEVEL	MEDICATION

November 1, 2019

INTENTION

GRATITUDE

MEDITATION	WEATHER	MOOD

TOO BAD THAT ALL THE PEOPLE WHO KNOW HOW TO RUN THE COUNTRY ARE
BUSY DRIVING TAXICABS AND CUTTING HAIR. - GEORGE BURNS

SLEEP	CYCLE	WATER
THRONE	OBSTACLES	INDULGENCES
EXERCISE	STRESS LEVEL	MEDICATION

ELEMENT		SEASON

♏ SCORPIO

November 2, 2019

INTENTION		GRATITUDE

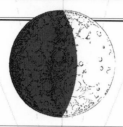

MEDITATION	WEATHER	MOOD

HOW A PERSON SEEMS TO SHOW UP FOR US IS INTIMATELY CONNECTED TO
HOW WE CHOOSE TO SHOW UP FOR THEM. - MARIANNE WILLIAMSON

SLEEP	CYCLE	WATER
THRONE	OBSTACLES	INDULGENCES
EXERCISE	STRESS LEVEL	MEDICATION

ELEMENT			SEASON
	 SCORPIO		

November 3, 2019

INTENTION		GRATITUDE
	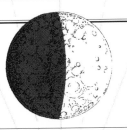	

MEDITATION	WEATHER	MOOD

A WOMAN IN HARMONY WITH HER SPIRIT IS LIKE A RIVER FLOWING. SHE GOES
WHERE SHE WILL WITHOUT PRETENSE AND ARRIVES AT HER DESTINATION
PREPARED TO BE HERSELF AND ONLY HERSELF. - MAYA ANGELOU

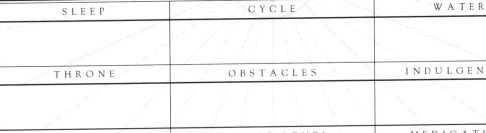

SLEEP	CYCLE	WATER
THRONE	OBSTACLES	INDULGENCES
EXERCISE	STRESS LEVEL	MEDICATION

ELEMENT		SEASON
	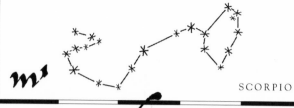 SCORPIO	

November 4, 2019

INTENTION	GRATITUDE

MEDITATION	WEATHER	MOOD

HERE IS THE AMAZING THING: THE CATERPILLAR AND THE BUTTERFLY HAVE THE EXACT SAME DNA. THEY ARE THE SAME ORGANISM BUT ARE RECEIVING AND RESPONDING TO A DIFFERENT ORGANIZING SIGNAL. - DR. BRUCE LIPTON

SLEEP	CYCLE	WATER
THRONE	OBSTACLES	INDULGENCES
EXERCISE	STRESS LEVEL	MEDICATION

November 5, 2019

INTENTION		GRATITUDE
	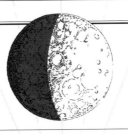	

MEDITATION	WEATHER	MOOD

I'M PAST PATIENTLY WAITIN' I'M PASSIONATELY SMASHIN' EVERY EXPECTATION. EVERY ACTION'S AN ACT OF CREATION. I'M LAUGHIN' IN THE FACE OF CASUALTIES AND SORROW. FOR THE FIRST TIME, I'M THINKIN' PAST TOMORROW. - LIN-MANUEL MIRANDA

SLEEP	CYCLE	WATER
THRONE	OBSTACLES	INDULGENCES
EXERCISE	STRESS LEVEL	MEDICATION

ELEMENT		SEASON
	 SCORPIO	

November 6, 2019

INTENTION		GRATITUDE

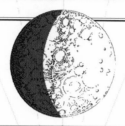

MEDITATION	WEATHER	MOOD

AND I AM NOT THROWING AWAY MY SHOT.
- LIN-MANUEL MIRANDA

SLEEP	CYCLE	WATER
THRONE	OBSTACLES	INDULGENCES
EXERCISE	STRESS LEVEL	MEDICATION

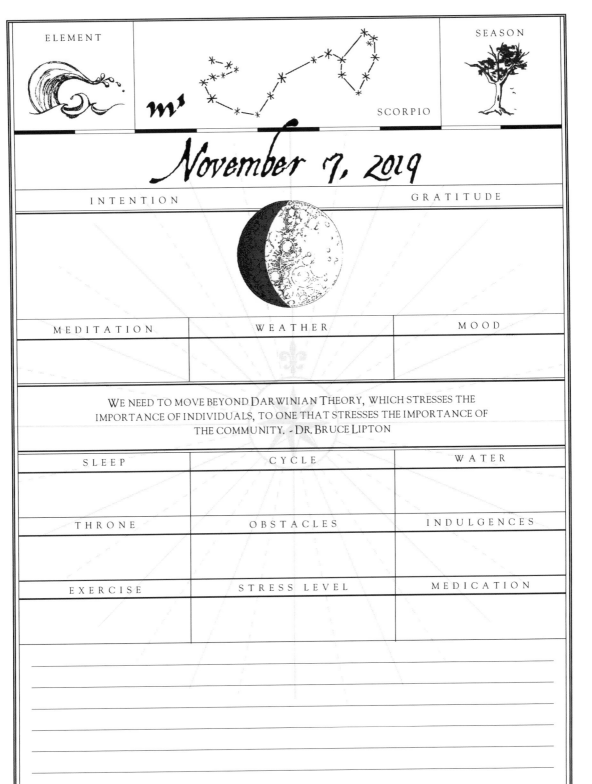

ELEMENT

SEASON

SCORPIO

November 7, 2019

INTENTION		GRATITUDE

MEDITATION	WEATHER	MOOD

WE NEED TO MOVE BEYOND DARWINIAN THEORY, WHICH STRESSES THE
IMPORTANCE OF INDIVIDUALS, TO ONE THAT STRESSES THE IMPORTANCE OF
THE COMMUNITY. - DR. BRUCE LIPTON

SLEEP	CYCLE	WATER

THRONE	OBSTACLES	INDULGENCES

EXERCISE	STRESS LEVEL	MEDICATION

ELEMENT			SEASON

 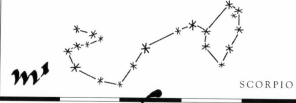 

m'

SCORPIO

November 8, 2019

INTENTION		GRATITUDE

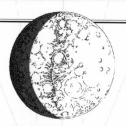

MEDITATION	WEATHER	MOOD

THIS IS NOT A MOMENT IT'S THE MOVEMENT.
- LIN-MANUEL MIRANDA

SLEEP	CYCLE	WATER
THRONE	OBSTACLES	INDULGENCES
EXERCISE	STRESS LEVEL	MEDICATION

ELEMENT			SEASON
	♏	SCORPIO	

November 9, 2019

INTENTION		GRATITUDE

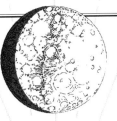

MEDITATION	WEATHER	MOOD

PHYSICISTS ABANDONED THEIR BELIEF IN A NEWTONIAN, MATERIAL UNIVERSE BECAUSE THEY HAD COME TO REALIZE THAT THE UNIVERSE IS NOT MADE OF MATTER SUSPENDED IN EMPTY SPACE BUT ENERGY. - DR. BRUCE LIPTON

SLEEP	CYCLE	WATER
THRONE	OBSTACLES	INDULGENCES
EXERCISE	STRESS LEVEL	MEDICATION

ELEMENT		SEASON

♏

SCORPIO

November 10, 2019

INTENTION		GRATITUDE

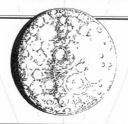

MEDITATION	WEATHER	MOOD

WOMEN ARE STILL IN EMOTIONAL BONDAGE AS LONG AS WE NEED TO WORRY THAT
WE MIGHT HAVE TO MAKE A CHOICE BETWEEN BEING HEARD AND BEING LOVED.
- MARIANNE WILLIAMSON

SLEEP	CYCLE	WATER
THRONE	OBSTACLES	INDULGENCES
EXERCISE	STRESS LEVEL	MEDICATION

ELEMENT		SEASON

SCORPIO

November 11, 2019

INTENTION		GRATITUDE

MEDITATION	WEATHER	MOOD

RISE UP. WHEN YOU'RE LIVING ON YOUR KNEES, YOU RISE UP. TELL YOUR BROTHER
THAT HE'S GOTTA RISE UP. TELL YOUR SISTER THAT SHE'S GOTTA RISE UP.
-LIN-MANUEL MIRANDA

SLEEP	CYCLE	WATER
THRONE	OBSTACLES	INDULGENCES
EXERCISE	STRESS LEVEL	MEDICATION

ELEMENT		SEASON
	 ♏ SCORPIO	

November 12, 2019

INTENTION		GRATITUDE

MEDITATION	WEATHER	MOOD

TOO OFTEN WE WOMEN TRY TO TACKLE CHAOS THAT IS NOT OURS TO FIX.
- AMY POEHLER

SLEEP	CYCLE	WATER

THRONE	OBSTACLES	INDULGENCES

EXERCISE	STRESS LEVEL	MEDICATION

m' SCORPIO

November 13, 2019

| INTENTION | | GRATITUDE |

| MEDITATION | WEATHER | MOOD |

A GREAT PARADOX OF CONTEMPORARY THERAPY IS THAT IT CRACKS OPEN SO
MANY CRISES OF THE MIND THAT CAN'T BE HEALED WITH THE MIND.
- CAROLINE MYSS

| SLEEP | CYCLE | WATER |

| THRONE | OBSTACLES | INDULGENCES |

| EXERCISE | STRESS LEVEL | MEDICATION |

ELEMENT			SEASON

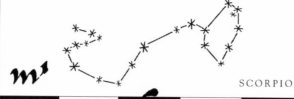

SCORPIO

November 14, 2019

INTENTION		GRATITUDE

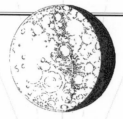

MEDITATION	WEATHER	MOOD

THOUGHT IS CAUSE; EXPERIENCE IS EFFECT. IF YOU DON'T LIKE THE EFFECTS IN
YOUR LIFE, YOU HAVE TO CHANGE THE NATURE OF YOUR THINKING.
- MARIANNE WILLIAMSON

SLEEP	CYCLE	WATER
THRONE	OBSTACLES	INDULGENCES
EXERCISE	STRESS LEVEL	MEDICATION

ELEMENT		SEASON
 ♏ SCORPIO		

November 15, 2019

INTENTION		GRATITUDE
	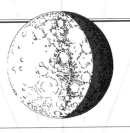	

MEDITATION	WEATHER	MOOD

WHEN YOU BUY INTO ANY VERSION OF FEAR, IT CAN BECOME YOUR EXPERIENCE BECAUSE YOUR MOLECULES ARE INTELLIGENT AND YOUR ENERGY RESPONDS TO THE PREDOMINANT FEELING IN YOUR BEING. THE FOCUS OF YOUR MIND IS EXACTLY WHAT GIVES THE ORDERS TO CREATE WHAT YOU EXPERIENCE. - BARBARA MARCINIAK

SLEEP	CYCLE	WATER

THRONE	OBSTACLES	INDULGENCES

EXERCISE	STRESS LEVEL	MEDICATION

_____
_____
_____
_____
_____
_____
_____
_____
_____
_____

ELEMENT		SCORPIO	SEASON

November 16, 2019

INTENTION		GRATITUDE

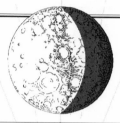

MEDITATION	WEATHER	MOOD

TRY TO BE A RAINBOW IN SOMEONE'S CLOUD.
- MAYA ANGELOU

SLEEP	CYCLE	WATER
THRONE	OBSTACLES	INDULGENCES
EXERCISE	STRESS LEVEL	MEDICATION

ELEMENT		SEASON

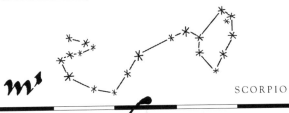

m'

SCORPIO

November 17, 2019

INTENTION		GRATITUDE

MEDITATION	WEATHER	MOOD

YOUR ABILITY TO NAVIGATE AND TOLERATE CHANGE AND ITS PAINFUL UNCOMFORTABLENESS DIRECTLY CORRELATES TO YOUR HAPPINESS AND GENERAL WELL-BEING. SEE WHAT I JUST DID THERE? I SAVED YOU THOUSANDS OF DOLLARS ON SELF-HELP BOOKS. IF YOU CAN SURF YOUR LIFE RATHER THAN PLANT YOUR FEET, YOU WILL BE HAPPIER. - AMY POEHLER

SLEEP	CYCLE	WATER
THRONE	OBSTACLES	INDULGENCES
EXERCISE	STRESS LEVEL	MEDICATION

ELEMENT			SEASON

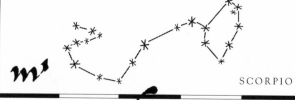

m̷ SCORPIO

November 18, 2019

INTENTION		GRATITUDE

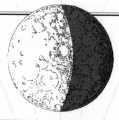

MEDITATION	WEATHER	MOOD

IF OUR EMOTIONAL STABILITY IS BASED ON WHAT OTHER PEOPLE DO OR DO
NOT DO, THEN WE HAVE NO STABILITY. IF OUR EMOTIONAL STABILITY IS BASED
ON LOVE THAT IS CHANGELESS AND UNALTERABLE, THEN WE ATTAIN THE
STABILITY OF GOD. - MARIANNE WILLIAMSON

SLEEP	CYCLE	WATER
THRONE	OBSTACLES	INDULGENCES
EXERCISE	STRESS LEVEL	MEDICATION

November 19, 2019

INTENTION

GRATITUDE

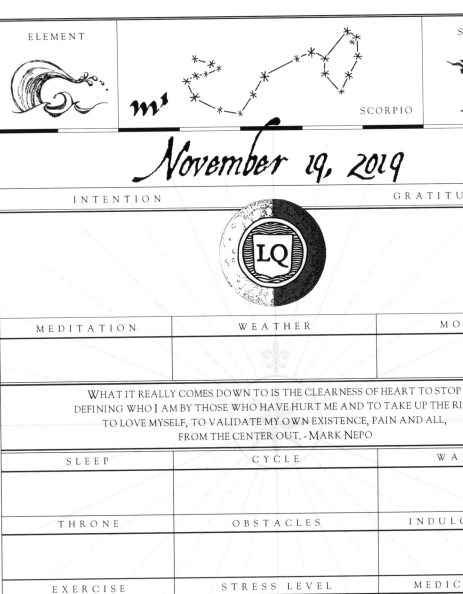

MEDITATION	WEATHER	MOOD

WHAT IT REALLY COMES DOWN TO IS THE CLEARNESS OF HEART TO STOP
DEFINING WHO I AM BY THOSE WHO HAVE HURT ME AND TO TAKE UP THE RISK
TO LOVE MYSELF, TO VALIDATE MY OWN EXISTENCE, PAIN AND ALL,
FROM THE CENTER OUT. - MARK NEPO

SLEEP	CYCLE	WATER
THRONE	OBSTACLES	INDULGENCES
EXERCISE	STRESS LEVEL	MEDICATION

ELEMENT		SEASON
	 SCORPIO	

November 20, 2019

INTENTION		GRATITUDE
	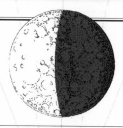	

MEDITATION	WEATHER	MOOD

WHEN YOU DO NOT SEEK OR NEED EXTERNAL APPROVAL, YOU ARE AT YOUR
MOST POWERFUL. - CAROLINE MYSS

SLEEP	CYCLE	WATER
THRONE	OBSTACLES	INDULGENCES
EXERCISE	STRESS LEVEL	MEDICATION

ELEMENT		SEASON
	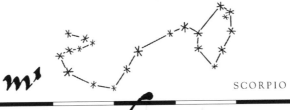 SCORPIO	

November 21, 2019

INTENTION		GRATITUDE
	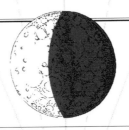	

MEDITATION	WEATHER	MOOD

 WHETHER OR NOT WE KNOW WHAT WE ARE CREATING OR HOW WE ARE CREATING IT, WHEN THINGS DO NOT TURN OUT THE WAY WE DESIRE, OUR HUMAN INSTINCTS DRIVE US TO LOOK FOR SOMEONE TO BLAME.
- IYANLA VANZANT

SLEEP	CYCLE	WATER
THRONE	OBSTACLES	INDULGENCES
EXERCISE	STRESS LEVEL	MEDICATION

_____
_____
_____
_____
_____
_____
_____
_____
_____
_____
_____

Sagittarius

November 22 – December 20

ELEMENT: FIRE

QUALITY: MUTABLE

RULING PLANET: JUPITER

CONSTELLATION: THE ARCHER

MODE: INTUITION

MOTTO: "I PHILOSOPHIZE"

IN THE GRAND CYCLE OF LIFE: 56-63 YEARS

THEMES:
EXPANSION, OPTIMISM, EXCESS,
FREEDOM, EXPLORATION,
PERSONAL & UNIVERSAL CONCERNS, IDEALISM

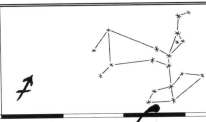
November 22, 2019

INTENTION		GRATITUDE
	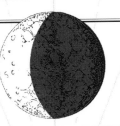	

MEDITATION	WEATHER	MOOD

LIFE IS PURE ADVENTURE, AND THE SOONER WE REALIZE THAT, THE QUICKER
WE WILL BE ABLE TO TREAT LIFE AS ART. - MAYA ANGELOU

SLEEP	CYCLE	WATER
THRONE	OBSTACLES	INDULGENCES
EXERCISE	STRESS LEVEL	MEDICATION

ELEMENT				SEASON

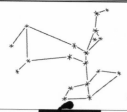

↗

SAGITTARIUS

November 23, 2019

INTENTION		GRATITUDE

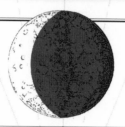

MEDITATION	WEATHER	MOOD

JUST LIKE A SINGLE CELL, THE CHARACTER OF OUR LIVES IS DETERMINED NOT
BY OUR GENES BUT BY OUR RESPONSES TO THE ENVIRONMENTAL SIGNALS
THAT PROPEL LIFE. - DR. BRUCE LIPTON

SLEEP	CYCLE	WATER
THRONE	OBSTACLES	INDULGENCES
EXERCISE	STRESS LEVEL	MEDICATION

ELEMENT			SEASON
	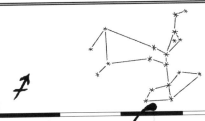♐	SAGITTARIUS	

November 29, 2019

INTENTION		GRATITUDE
	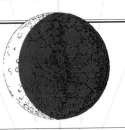	

MEDITATION	WEATHER	MOOD

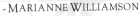

THE WAY OF THE MIRACLE-WORKER IS TO SEE ALL HUMAN BEHAVIOR AS ONE
OF TWO THINGS: EITHER LOVE, OR A CALL FOR LOVE.
- MARIANNE WILLIAMSON

SLEEP	CYCLE	WATER
THRONE	OBSTACLES	INDULGENCES
EXERCISE	STRESS LEVEL	MEDICATION

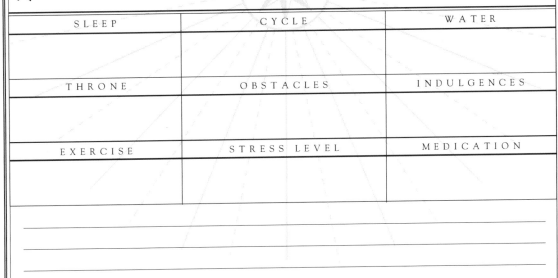

ELEMENT			SEASON

 ♐ 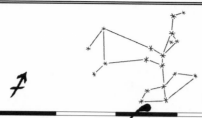 SAGITTARIUS

November 25, 2019

INTENTION		GRATITUDE

MEDITATION	WEATHER	MOOD

NEW MOON HEADS UP! CENTER YOUR INTENTIONS AROUND: ADVENTURE, EXPANSION, TRAVEL, OPTIMISM & FREEDOM

SLEEP	CYCLE	WATER
THRONE	OBSTACLES	INDULGENCES
EXERCISE	STRESS LEVEL	MEDICATION

New Moon Intentions

ELEMENT			SEASON

♐

SAGITTARIUS

November 26, 2019

INTENTION		GRATITUDE

MEDITATION	WEATHER	MOOD

BIOLOGICAL BEHAVIOR CAN BE CONTROLLED BY INVISIBLE FORCES, INCLUDING
THOUGHT, AS WELL AS IT CAN BE CONTROLLED BY PHYSICAL MOLECULES LIKE
PENICILLIN, A FACT THAT PROVIDES THE SCIENTIFIC UNDERPINNING FOR
PHARMACEUTICAL-FREE ENERGY MEDICINE. - DR. BRUCE LIPTON

SLEEP	CYCLE	WATER
THRONE	OBSTACLES	INDULGENCES
EXERCISE	STRESS LEVEL	MEDICATION

ELEMENT			SEASON
	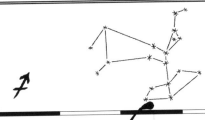 ♐	SAGITTARIUS	

November 27, 2019

INTENTION		GRATITUDE

MEDITATION	WEATHER	MOOD

LOVE IS THE FUEL OF OUR PHYSICAL AND SPIRITUAL BODIES.
- CAROLINE MYSS

SLEEP	CYCLE	WATER
THRONE	OBSTACLES	INDULGENCES
EXERCISE	STRESS LEVEL	MEDICATION

ELEMENT			SEASON
	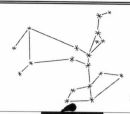		
	↗	SAGITTARIUS	

November 28, 2019

INTENTION		GRATITUDE

MEDITATION	WEATHER	MOOD

THAT WHICH IS USED - DEVELOPS. THAT WHICH IS NOT USED WASTES AWAY.
- HIPPOCRATES

SLEEP	CYCLE	WATER
THRONE	OBSTACLES	INDULGENCES
EXERCISE	STRESS LEVEL	MEDICATION

_____
_____
_____
_____
_____
_____
_____
_____
_____
_____

ELEMENT		SEASON
	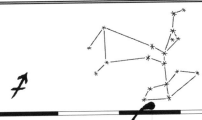 ♐ SAGITTARIUS	

November 29, 2019

INTENTION		GRATITUDE

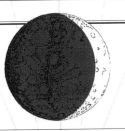

MEDITATION	WEATHER	MOOD

NOTHING BINDS YOU EXCEPT YOUR THOUGHTS; NOTHING LIMITS YOU EXCEPT
YOUR FEAR; AND NOTHING CONTROLS YOU EXCEPT YOUR BELIEFS.
- MARIANNE WILLIAMSON

SLEEP	CYCLE	WATER
THRONE	OBSTACLES	INDULGENCES
EXERCISE	STRESS LEVEL	MEDICATION

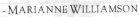

ELEMENT		SAGITTARIUS		SEASON
	♐ 			

November 30, 2019

INTENTION		GRATITUDE
	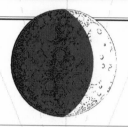	

MEDITATION	WEATHER	MOOD

THE SHOW DOESN'T GO ON BECAUSE IT'S READY; IT GOES ON BECAUSE IT'S 11:30.
- TINA FEY

SLEEP	CYCLE	WATER
THRONE	OBSTACLES	INDULGENCES
EXERCISE	STRESS LEVEL	MEDICATION

ELEMENT		SEASON
	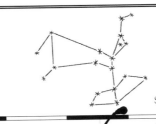 ♐ SAGITTARIUS	

December 1, 2019

INTENTION	GRATITUDE

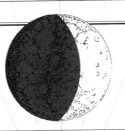

MEDITATION	WEATHER	MOOD

 EVERYONE WANTS TO RIDE WITH YOU IN THE LIMO, BUT WHAT YOU WANT IS SOMEONE WHO WILL TAKE THE BUS WITH YOU WHEN THE LIMO BREAKS DOWN. - OPRAH

SLEEP	CYCLE	WATER
THRONE	OBSTACLES	INDULGENCES
EXERCISE	STRESS LEVEL	MEDICATION

ELEMENT		SEASON

♐

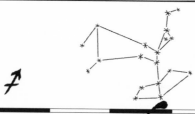

SAGITTARIUS

December 2, 2019

INTENTION		GRATITUDE

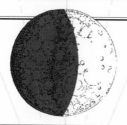

MEDITATION	WEATHER	MOOD

NOTHING CAN DIM THE LIGHT WHICH SHINES FROM WITHIN.
- MAYA ANGELOU

SLEEP	CYCLE	WATER
THRONE	OBSTACLES	INDULGENCES
EXERCISE	STRESS LEVEL	MEDICATION

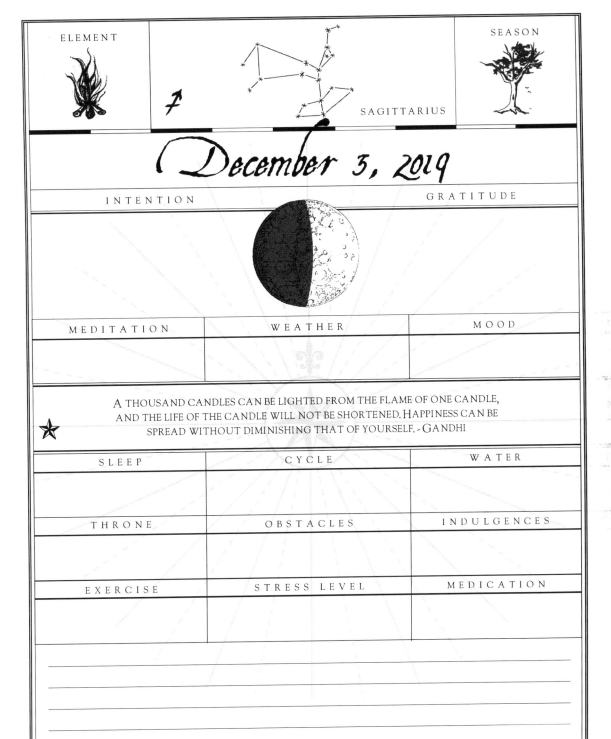

ELEMENT

SAGITTARIUS

SEASON

December 3, 2019

INTENTION   GRATITUDE

MEDITATION   WEATHER   MOOD

A THOUSAND CANDLES CAN BE LIGHTED FROM THE FLAME OF ONE CANDLE,
AND THE LIFE OF THE CANDLE WILL NOT BE SHORTENED. HAPPINESS CAN BE
SPREAD WITHOUT DIMINISHING THAT OF YOURSELF. - GANDHI

SLEEP   CYCLE   WATER

THRONE   OBSTACLES   INDULGENCES

EXERCISE   STRESS LEVEL   MEDICATION

ELEMENT			SEASON

↗

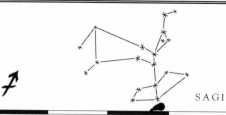

SAGITTARIUS

December 4, 2019

INTENTION		GRATITUDE

MEDITATION	WEATHER	MOOD

FOR THOSE WHO CONFUSE YOU, RECOGNIZE THAT THEIR CONFUSION IS THEIRS
AND YOUR CLARITY IS YOURS. - BARBARA MARCINIAK

SLEEP	CYCLE	WATER
THRONE	OBSTACLES	INDULGENCES
EXERCISE	STRESS LEVEL	MEDICATION

_____
_____
_____
_____
_____
_____
_____
_____
_____

ELEMENT			SEASON

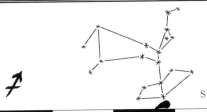

SAGITTARIUS

December 5, 2019

INTENTION		GRATITUDE

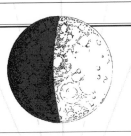

MEDITATION	WEATHER	MOOD

SURRENDER MEANS, BY DEFINITION, GIVING UP ATTACHMENT TO RESULTS.
WHEN WE SURRENDER TO GOD, WE LET GO OF OUR ATTACHMENT TO HOW
THINGS HAPPEN ON THE OUTSIDE AND WE BECOME MORE CONCERNED WITH
WHAT HAPPENS ON THE INSIDE. - MARIANNE WILLIAMSON

SLEEP	CYCLE	WATER
THRONE	OBSTACLES	INDULGENCES
EXERCISE	STRESS LEVEL	MEDICATION

ELEMENT				SEASON
	♐	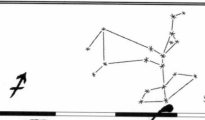 SAGITTARIUS		

December 6, 2019

INTENTION		GRATITUDE
	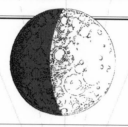	

MEDITATION	WEATHER	MOOD

BE PRESENT IN ALL THINGS AND THANKFUL FOR ALL THINGS.
- MAYA ANGLEOU

SLEEP	CYCLE	WATER
THRONE	OBSTACLES	INDULGENCES
EXERCISE	STRESS LEVEL	MEDICATION

ELEMENT			SEASON

♐

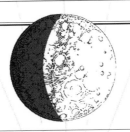

SAGITTARIUS

December 7, 2019

INTENTION		GRATITUDE

MEDITATION	WEATHER	MOOD

THE QUANTUM MODEL, WHICH STATES THAT ALL POSSIBILITIES EXIST IN THIS
PRESENT MOMENT, IS YOUR KEY TO USING THE PLACEBO EFFECT FOR HEALING,
BECAUSE IT GIVES YOU PERMISSION TO CHOOSE A NEW FUTURE FOR YOURSELF
AND ACTUALLY OBSERVE IT INTO REALITY.- JOE DISPENZA

SLEEP	CYCLE	WATER
THRONE	OBSTACLES	INDULGENCES
EXERCISE	STRESS LEVEL	MEDICATION

ELEMENT		SAGITTARIUS		SEASON

December 8, 2019

INTENTION	GRATITUDE

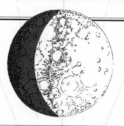

MEDITATION	WEATHER	MOOD

MY MISSION IN LIFE IS NOT MERELY TO SURVIVE, BUT TO THRIVE; AND TO DO
SO WITH SOME PASSION, SOME COMPASSION, SOME HUMOR, AND SOME STYLE.
- MAYA ANGELOU

SLEEP	CYCLE	WATER
THRONE	OBSTACLES	INDULGENCES
EXERCISE	STRESS LEVEL	MEDICATION

_____
_____
_____
_____
_____
_____
_____
_____
_____
_____

ELEMENT		SEASON
	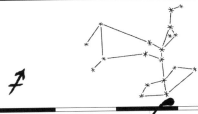 ♐ SAGITTARIUS	

December 9, 2019

INTENTION		GRATITUDE

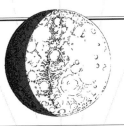

MEDITATION	WEATHER	MOOD

THE SOUL ALWAYS KNOWS WHAT TO DO TO HEAL ITSELF. THE CHALLENGE IS
TO SILENCE THE MIND. - CAROLINE MYSS

SLEEP	CYCLE	WATER
THRONE	OBSTACLES	INDULGENCES
EXERCISE	STRESS LEVEL	MEDICATION

ELEMENT			SEASON
	♐	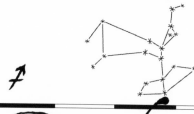 SAGITTARIUS	

December 10, 2019

INTENTION		GRATITUDE
	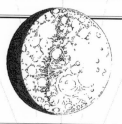	

MEDITATION	WEATHER	MOOD

★ THE ONLY WAY TO CONSCIOUSLY DEACTIVATE A THOUGHT IS TO ACTIVATE ANOTHER. IN OTHER WORDS, THE ONLY WAY TO DELIBERATELY WITHDRAW YOUR ATTENTION FROM ONE THOUGHT IS TO GIVE YOUR ATTENTION TO ANOTHER. - ABRAHAM/HICKS

SLEEP	CYCLE	WATER
THRONE	OBSTACLES	INDULGENCES
EXERCISE	STRESS LEVEL	MEDICATION

ELEMENT		SAGITTARIUS	SEASON

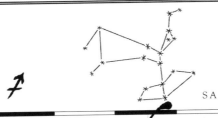

December 11, 2019

INTENTION	GRATITUDE

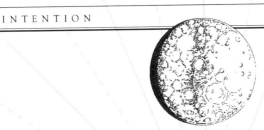

MEDITATION	WEATHER	MOOD

RAISE YOUR WORDS, NOT VOICE. IT IS RAIN THAT GROWS FLOWERS, NOT THUNDER.
- RUMI

SLEEP	CYCLE	WATER
THRONE	OBSTACLES	INDULGENCES
EXERCISE	STRESS LEVEL	MEDICATION

ELEMENT		SEASON
	 ♐ SAGITTARIUS	

December 12, 2019

INTENTION		GRATITUDE

MEDITATION	WEATHER	MOOD

 ALL THAT WAS GREAT IN THE PAST WAS RIDICULED, CONDEMNED, COMBATED, SUPPRESSED — ONLY TO EMERGE ALL THE MORE POWERFULLY, ALL THE MORE TRIUMPHANTLY FROM THE STRUGGLE. - NIKOLA TESLA

SLEEP	CYCLE	WATER
THRONE	OBSTACLES	INDULGENCES
EXERCISE	STRESS LEVEL	MEDICATION

ELEMENT			SEASON
	♐	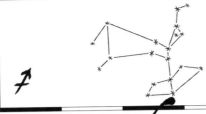 SAGITTARIUS	

December 13, 2019

INTENTION		GRATITUDE
	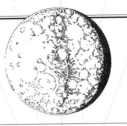	

MEDITATION	WEATHER	MOOD

WHEN YOU CAN LOOK A THING DEAD IN THE EYE, ACKNOWLEDGE THAT IT
EXISTS, CALL IT EXACTLY WHAT IT IS, AND DECIDE WHAT ROLE IT WILL TAKE
IN YOUR LIFE THEN, MY BELOVED, YOU HAVE TAKEN THE FIRST STEP TOWARD
YOUR FREEDOM. - IYANLA VANZANT

SLEEP	CYCLE	WATER
THRONE	OBSTACLES	INDULGENCES
EXERCISE	STRESS LEVEL	MEDICATION

ELEMENT		SAGITTARIUS	SEASON

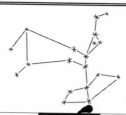

December 4, 2019

INTENTION		GRATITUDE

MEDITATION	WEATHER	MOOD

YOUR THOUGHTS ARE INCREDIBLY POWERFUL. CHOOSE YOURS WISELY.
- JOE DISPENZA

SLEEP	CYCLE	WATER
THRONE	OBSTACLES	INDULGENCES
EXERCISE	STRESS LEVEL	MEDICATION

ELEMENT			SEASON
	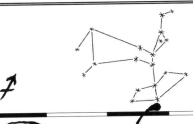 ♐ SAGITTARIUS		

December 15, 2019

INTENTION	GRATITUDE

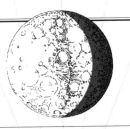

MEDITATION	WEATHER	MOOD

HAVE ENOUGH COURAGE TO TRUST LOVE ONE MORE TIME AND ALWAYS ONE MORE TIME.
-MAYA ANGELOU

SLEEP	CYCLE	WATER
THRONE	OBSTACLES	INDULGENCES
EXERCISE	STRESS LEVEL	MEDICATION

ELEMENT			SEASON
	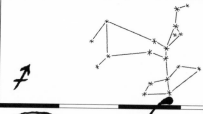 ↗ SAGITTARIUS		

December 16, 2019

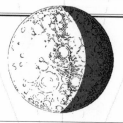

INTENTION		GRATITUDE

MEDITATION	WEATHER	MOOD

 YOUR TASK IS NOT TO SEEK FOR LOVE, BUT MERELY TO SEEK AND FIND ALL THE
BARRIERS WITHIN YOURSELF THAT YOU HAVE BUILT AGAINST IT. - RUMI

SLEEP	CYCLE	WATER
THRONE	OBSTACLES	INDULGENCES
EXERCISE	STRESS LEVEL	MEDICATION

_____
_____
_____
_____
_____
_____
_____
_____
_____
_____

ELEMENT		SAGITTARIUS	SEASON

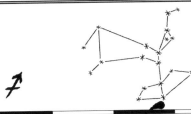

December 17, 2019

INTENTION		GRATITUDE

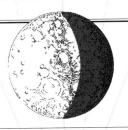

MEDITATION	WEATHER	MOOD

AS LONG AS WE REMAIN VIGILANT AT BUILDING OUR INTERNAL
ABUNDANCE— AN ABUNDANCE OF INTEGRITY, AN ABUNDANCE OF
FORGIVENESS, AN ABUNDANCE OF SERVICE, AN ABUNDANCE OF LOVE— THEN
EXTERNAL LACK IS BOUND TO BE TEMPORARY. - MARIANNE WILLIAMSON

SLEEP	CYCLE	WATER
THRONE	OBSTACLES	INDULGENCES
EXERCISE	STRESS LEVEL	MEDICATION

ELEMENT		SAGITTARIUS	SEASON
	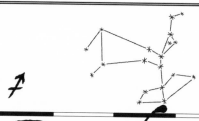		

December 18, 2019

INTENTION		GRATITUDE

MEDITATION	WEATHER	MOOD

YOU NEED TO LEARN HOW TO SELECT YOUR THOUGHTS JUST THE SAME WAY YOU SELECT YOUR CLOTHES EVERY DAY. THIS IS A POWER YOU CAN CULTIVATE. IF YOU WANT TO CONTROL THINGS IN YOUR LIFE SO BAD, WORK ON THE MIND. THAT'S THE ONLY THING YOU SHOULD BE TRYING TO CONTROL. - ELIZABETH GILBERT

SLEEP	CYCLE	WATER
THRONE	OBSTACLES	INDULGENCES
EXERCISE	STRESS LEVEL	MEDICATION

ELEMENT		SAGITTARIUS		SEASON
	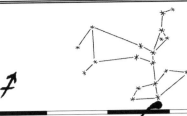			

December 19, 2019

INTENTION		GRATITUDE
	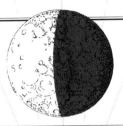	

MEDITATION	WEATHER	MOOD

THE UNIVERSE IS ONE INDIVISIBLE, DYNAMIC WHOLE IN WHICH ENERGY AND MATTER ARE SO DEEPLY ENTANGLED IT IS IMPOSSIBLE TO CONSIDER THEM AS INDEPENDENT ELEMENTS. - DR. BRUCE LIPTON

SLEEP	CYCLE	WATER
THRONE	OBSTACLES	INDULGENCES
EXERCISE	STRESS LEVEL	MEDICATION

ELEMENT			SEASON
	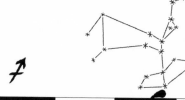	 SAGITTARIUS	

December 20, 2019

INTENTION		GRATITUDE

MEDITATION	WEATHER	MOOD

SUCCESS IS LIKING YOURSELF, LIKING WHAT YOU DO, AND LIKING HOW YOU DO IT.
- MAYA ANGELOU

SLEEP	CYCLE	WATER
THRONE	OBSTACLES	INDULGENCES
EXERCISE	STRESS LEVEL	MEDICATION

Capricorn

December 21 – January 19

ELEMENT: EARTH

QUALITY: CARDINAL

RULING PLANET: SATURN

CONSTELLATION: THE GOAT

MODE: SENSATION

MOTTO: "I MASTER"

IN THE GRAND CYCLE OF LIFE: 63-70 YEARS

THEMES:
AMBITION, SUCCESS, CRYSTALLIZATION OF THOUGHTS & IDEAS,
MATURITY, RESPONSIBILITY, FATE, INFLEXIBILITY

ELEMENT		CAPRICORN	SEASON

 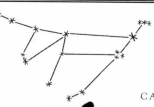

December 21, 2019

INTENTION		GRATITUDE

 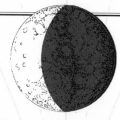 *Winter* *Solstice*

MEDITATION	WEATHER	MOOD

 ATTITUDES STRUNG TOGETHER BECOME BELIEFS, AND RELATED BELIEFS STRUNG TOGETHER BECOME PERCEPTIONS. OVER TIME, THIS REDUNDANCY CREATES A VIEW OF THE WORLD AND OF YOURSELF THAT'S LARGELY SUBCONSCIOUS. - JOE DISPENZA

SLEEP	CYCLE	WATER
THRONE	OBSTACLES	INDULGENCES
EXERCISE	STRESS LEVEL	MEDICATION

ELEMENT			SEASON

ꡃ CAPRICORN

December 22, 2019

INTENTION		GRATITUDE

MEDITATION	WEATHER	MOOD

IF YOU CAN DANCE AND BE FREE AND NOT EMBARRASSED YOU CAN RULE THE WORLD.
- AMY POEHLER

SLEEP	CYCLE	WATER
THRONE	OBSTACLES	INDULGENCES
EXERCISE	STRESS LEVEL	MEDICATION

ELEMENT		CAPRICORN	SEASON

December 23, 2019

INTENTION		GRATITUDE

MEDITATION	WEATHER	MOOD

IF YOU DO NOT FILL YOUR ENERGETIC FIELD WITH NEW EXPERIENCES, NEW
IDEAS, AND NEW VERSIONS OF YOURSELF, YOUR FIELD BECOMES DIM AND
WORN, BORED WITH THE SAME OLD STORY. - BARBARA MARCINIAK

SLEEP	CYCLE	WATER
THRONE	OBSTACLES	INDULGENCES
EXERCISE	STRESS LEVEL	MEDICATION

ELEMENT		CAPRICORN	SEASON

December 24, 2019

INTENTION		GRATITUDE

MEDITATION	WEATHER	MOOD

WHEN WE GIVE CHEERFULLY AND ACCEPT GRATEFULLY, EVERYONE IS BLESSED.
-MAYA ANGLEOU

SLEEP	CYCLE	WATER
THRONE	OBSTACLES	INDULGENCES
EXERCISE	STRESS LEVEL	MEDICATION

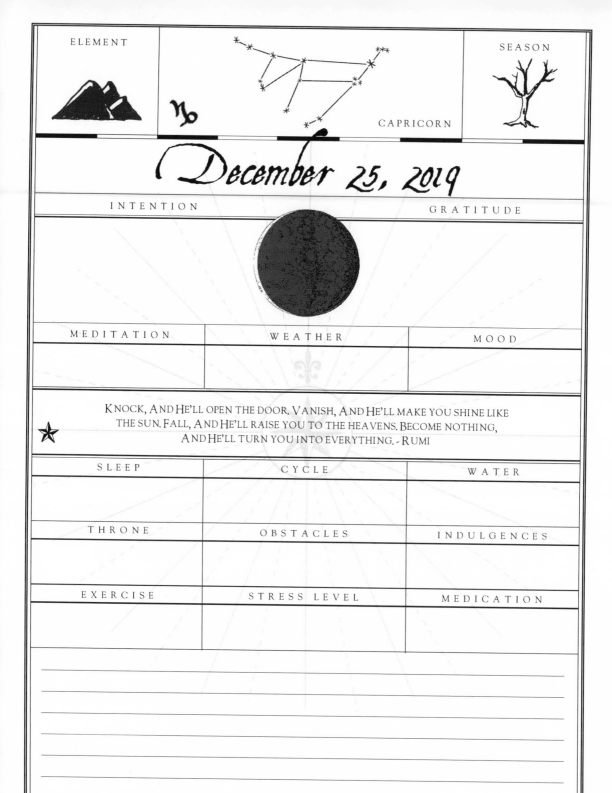

ELEMENT		CAPRICORN	SEASON

December 25, 2019

INTENTION	GRATITUDE

MEDITATION	WEATHER	MOOD

KNOCK, AND HE'LL OPEN THE DOOR. VANISH, AND HE'LL MAKE YOU SHINE LIKE
THE SUN. FALL, AND HE'LL RAISE YOU TO THE HEAVENS. BECOME NOTHING,
AND HE'LL TURN YOU INTO EVERYTHING. - RUMI

SLEEP	CYCLE	WATER
THRONE	OBSTACLES	INDULGENCES
EXERCISE	STRESS LEVEL	MEDICATION

The HMS Energy Wheel

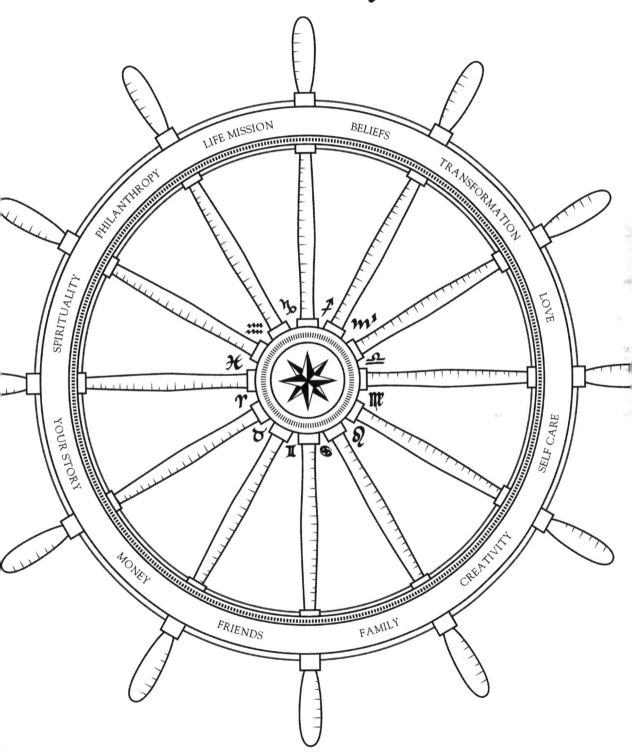

12/26 *New Moon Intentions* 12:13 AM EST

New Moon Intentions

ELEMENT				SEASON

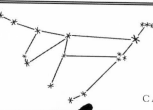

CAPRICORN

December 26, 2019

INTENTION	GRATITUDE

MEDITATION	WEATHER	MOOD

New Moon Heads Up! Center your Intentions around: Goals,
Ambition, Respect, Success, Accepting Responsibility, Taking Charge

SLEEP	CYCLE	WATER
THRONE	OBSTACLES	INDULGENCES
EXERCISE	STRESS LEVEL	MEDICATION

ELEMENT			SEASON

 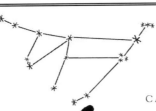

CAPRICORN

December 27, 2019

INTENTION		GRATITUDE

MEDITATION	WEATHER	MOOD

HAPPINESS IS HAVING A LARGE, LOVING, CARING, CLOSE-KNIT FAMILY IN ANOTHER CITY.
- GEORGE BURNS

SLEEP	CYCLE	WATER
THRONE	OBSTACLES	INDULGENCES
EXERCISE	STRESS LEVEL	MEDICATION

ELEMENT			SEASON
	♑	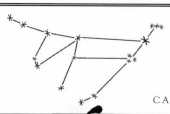 CAPRICORN	

December 28, 2019

INTENTION		GRATITUDE
	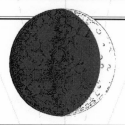	

MEDITATION	WEATHER	MOOD

YOU CAN ONLY BECOME TRULY ACCOMPLISHED AT SOMETHING YOU LOVE. DON'T MAKE MONEY YOUR GOAL. INSTEAD PURSUE THE THINGS YOU LOVE DOING AND THEN DO THEM SO WELL THAT PEOPLE CAN'T TAKE THEIR EYES OFF OF YOU. - MAYA ANGELOU

SLEEP	CYCLE	WATER
THRONE	OBSTACLES	INDULGENCES
EXERCISE	STRESS LEVEL	MEDICATION

December 29, 2019

INTENTION		GRATITUDE

MEDITATION	WEATHER	MOOD

SUCCESS MEANS WE GO TO SLEEP AT NIGHT KNOWING THAT OUR TALENTS AND ABILITIES WERE USED IN A WAY THAT SERVED OTHERS. - MARIANNE WILLIAMSON

SLEEP	CYCLE	WATER
THRONE	OBSTACLES	INDULGENCES
EXERCISE	STRESS LEVEL	MEDICATION

ELEMENT				SEASON
	♑	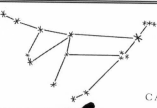	CAPRICORN	

December 30, 2019

INTENTION	GRATITUDE

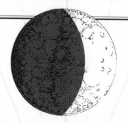

MEDITATION	WEATHER	MOOD

STOP ACTING SO SMALL, YOU ARE THE UNIVERSE IN ECSTATIC MOTION.
- RUMI

SLEEP	CYCLE	WATER
THRONE	OBSTACLES	INDULGENCES
EXERCISE	STRESS LEVEL	MEDICATION

ELEMENT			SEASON

♑ CAPRICORN

December 31, 2019

INTENTION		GRATITUDE

MEDITATION	WEATHER	MOOD

WE CAN'T CREATE A NEW FUTURE WHILE WE'RE LIVING IN OUR PAST.
IT'S SIMPLY IMPOSSIBLE. - JOE DISPENZA

SLEEP	CYCLE	WATER
THRONE	OBSTACLES	INDULGENCES
EXERCISE	STRESS LEVEL	MEDICATION

Bibliography

1. Varcas, Sarah. *Solar Eclipse in Taurus: 9th/10th May 2013* (12:30 a.m. GMT 10th). Complete text online at http://astro-awakenings.co.uk/solar-eclipse-in-taurus-9th10th-may-2013.

2. Desai, Dipali. *Full Moon and Lunar Eclipse in Scorpio April 25th*, 2013. Complete text online at http://celestialspace.wordpress.com/.

3. Pagano, Cathy. *The Cosmic Story: Aries/Libra Full Moon Eclipse, October 18, 2013: Eclipse Season Signals a Big Change Coming.* Complete text online at http://www.wisdom-of-astrology.com/astrostarsarticles/the-cosmic-story-aries-lunar-eclipse-october-18-2013.

4. Goldschneider, Gary, and Joost Elffers. *The Secret Language of Birthdays: Personality Profiles for Every Day of the Year.* New York: The Penguin Group, 1994.

5. Ibid.

6. Williams, Mark, and Danny Penman. Mindfulness: *An Eight-Week Plan for Finding Peace in a Frantic World.* Pennsylvania: Rodale Press, Inc., 2012.

7. Millman, Dan. *The Life You Were Born to Live: A Guide to Finding Your Life Purpose.* California: H. J. Kramer, Inc., 1995.

8. Dr. Maoshing Ni. *Secrets of Longevity, Hundreds of Ways to Live to Be 100.* California: Chronicle Books, 2006.

9. McDaniel, Douglas. *Archangel Michael Speaks!* Charleston, SC: Create Space Independent Publishing Platform, 2013.

10. Dr. Maoshing Ni. *Secrets of Longevity, Hundreds of Ways to Live to Be 100.* California: Chronicle Books, 2006.

11. Wordsworth, William. "The World Is Too Much with Us." *Poems, in Two Volumes,* London: Longman, Hurst, Rees, and Orme, 1807.

Acknowledgements

Special thanks to the many authors, spiritual leaders, healers and scientists whose ideas inspire each day of the HMS Log Book. This edition of the journal is filled primarily with those influencers, past and present, who focus on concepts of the energetic realm. It is my desire that the daily quotes will encourage you to dive deeper into the worlds of these celebrated minds so that a greater knowledge of these mysteries can be attained, thereby raising the vibration of all. When we endeavor to reclaim our energetic sovereignty, we can experience a shift towards freedom like no other, and the legends quoted in the HMS Log Book provide an endless well of information to help guide you on this journey. As the collective consciousness becomes more acquainted with the knowledge that our *attention* is the new currency, I invite you to be very selective about what you *pay attention* to. All the authors mentioned below are beyond worthy of your precious and sacred energy exchange.

Thank you to Marianne Williamson for her masterpiece, *A Return to Love*, as well as, *The Law of Divine Compensation*, *The Age of Miracles*, *Everyday Grace*, *A Woman's Worth*, *Illuminata*, *Healing the Soul of America*, *A Course in Weight Loss*, *The Gift of Change*, *Enchanted Love*, *A Year of Miracles*, and *Tears to Triumph: The Spiritual Journey from Suffering to Enlightenment*.

Thank you to Maya Angelou for her ground-breaking poetry, *I Know Why the Caged Bird Sings*, *Gather Together in My Name*, *The Heart of a Woman*, *A Song Flung Up to Heaven*, *All God's Children Need Traveling Shoes*, and *Mom & Me & Mom*.

Thank you to Barbara Marciniak for courageously publishing all that has been channeled from The Pleiadians with *Bringers of the Dawn: Teachings of the Pleiadians*, *Earth*, *Path of Empowerment* and *Family of Light*. Thank you to Esther & Jerry Hicks for the priceless volume of channeled information from the benevolent and enlightened *Abraham*.

Thank you to Iyanla Vanzant for her brilliant perspective in, *Peace from Broken Places*, *In the Meantime*, *One Day My Soul Just Opened Up*, *Yesterday I Cried*, *Acts of Faith: Meditations for People of Color*, *Forgiveness*, *The Spirit of a Man* and *Tapping the Power Within*. Thank you to Caroline Myss for her wealth of valuable information through, *Sacred Contracts*, *Your Power to Create*, *Navigating Hope*, *Three Levels of Power and How to Use Them*, *Energy Anatomy* and *Intuitive Power: Your Natural Resource*.

Thank you to Dr. Bruce Lipton for the life-changing read, *The Biology of Belief*. If you only read one more book in your entire life, make it this one.

Thank you to Amy Poehler, Tina Fey and Elizabeth Gilbert for their special combination of brilliance and humor. Thank you to Joe Dispenza and Mark Nepo for their beautiful inspiration. Thank you to Freddy Silva, Nikola Tesla, Rumi, Hippocrates, HH the Dalai Lama and Gandhi for the wonderful insight and enlightening research.

A very special thank you to Oprah Winfrey for her beautiful work and for bringing many of these powerful thought leaders the attention they deserve.

Endless gratitude and my undying love and affection to Lin-Manuel Miranda for his epic work of genius, *Hamilton*.

Notes

Notes

Notes

Notes

Notes

Notes

Notes

Notes

Notes

Notes

Notes

Notes

Notes

Notes

Notes

Notes

Notes

Notes

Notes

About the Author

Jen Snyder is a College of Charleston graduate who has spent most of her life in the quaint, Holy City of Charleston, SC, raising her daughter, working with the family business, singing in several bands and authoring the HMS Log Book series. In 2013 Jen was called to create a journal that would provide a safe and loving way to bring order, inspiration and loving accountability to the busy user. The first edition of the HMS Log Book launched in the Spring of 2014 and is a one of a kind, guided journaling experience with a unique fill-in-the-blank format. Life coaches, therapists and doctors love recommending this wonderful journal.

Jen offers workshops and group sessions that are designed to inspire a lasting self-care practice with the HMS Log Book as the foundation. She also works with young women in the local High Schools and Middle Schools presenting her Female Empowerment Program. This ongoing workshop series is designed to bring teenagers into a safe space where they can connect to and accept all parts of themselves while learning new and exciting ways to support themselves and each other without judgement, shame or guilt. With a healthy sense of humor and a toolbox chock full of high vibrational empowerment tools, she draws on her 21 years of parenting skills in helping guide women of all ages to the Self-Care Revolution.

Made in the USA
Columbia, SC
08 June 2019